Critical Guides to German Texts

D0220070

8 Schiller: Maria Stuart

Critical Guides to German Texts

EDITED BY MARTIN SWALES

SCHILLER

Maria Stuart

Erika Swales

Fellow of King's College, Cambridge

Grant & Cutler Ltd
1988

© Grant & Cutler Ltd
1988
ISBN 0 7293 0298 9

I.S.B.N. 84-599-2546-3

DEPÓSITO LEGAL: V. 2.675 - 1988

Printed in Spain by
Artes Gráficas Soler, S.A., Valencia
for
GRANT & CUTLER LTD
55-57, GREAT MARLBOROUGH STREET, LONDON W1V 2AY

for Christopher and Catherine

Contents

Prefatory Note

Quotations from *Maria Stuart* list as their source the appropriate line numbers. Quotations from other works by Schiller are taken from the *Nationalausgabe,* which is abbreviated to NA, followed by the volume number in Roman numerals and then the page number. Letters are also quoted from the *Nationalausgabe.* References to secondary literature appear as italicised figures, which correspond to the numbered items in the Select Bibliography.

This study has emerged from a whole number of supervision sessions which over the years have been a feature of my teaching at King's College Cambridge. I am profoundly grateful to all those undergraduates who have worked on the play with me. Their energy, enthusiasm and perception has helped me more than I can say.

Introduction

Beneath the clarity of its formal and philosophical design, Schiller's *Maria Stuart* is, in my view, a highly complex play. The short format of a *Critical Guide* does not allow for a detailed discussion of the many critical issues which the text raises, but I hope that my comments will enable the reader to have a fresh look at the play.

This study pays particular attention to the many and densely interrelated levels that make up the play's formal organization. I would argue that *Maria Stuart* is marked by that multi-faceted structure and multi-dimensionality which Wilkinson and Willoughby perceive at the centre of Schiller's *Aesthetic Education of Man.* I am above all concerned with the question how the interplay of various levels and perspectives affects our evaluation of the characters and, especially, of the play's status as a tragedy.

As is commonly known, after his encounter with Kant's *Kritik der praktischen Vernunft* and *Kritik der Urteilskraft,* Schiller comes to define the function of tragedy as the illumination of our capability to overcome physical nature, to exercise in the name of the moral law our own free will. The suffering and ultimate triumph which this regenerative process entails for the tragic protagonist is to elicit from the reader and spectator the responses of pity and admiration. The fate of Maria and the development she undergoes are generally seen as a brilliantly clear demonstration of these very tenets. In fact, the play is often criticized for being all too clear, too perfect in its translation of theory into practice. I have no wish to deny that the tragic fate of Maria can and does elicit the responses of pity and admiration. But I seek to show that the text with its highly sophisticated interplay of shifting perspectives demands a more differentiated response, a mode of complex seeing. Time and again we are invited both to judge and to reflect on the conditions of our judgment. Neither pity nor admiration are left

as simple, unquestioned responses, exempt from other,
competing reactions. In this sense the play seems to me to be
closer to our modern sense of scepticism and uncertainty than
has commonly been allowed.

1. Genesis and Critical Reception

The composition of the *Wallenstein* trilogy, which was finally completed on 17 March 1799, had brought Schiller to the brink of utter exhaustion. And yet, amazingly, the creative urge persisted. Two days later, on March 19th, Schiller writes to Goethe that he is tired of the world of 'Soldaten, Helden und Herrscher' (NA XXX, p.47); but even so the realm of history and politics retains its hold over him: he begins to study the reign of Elizabeth and perceives in the trial of Mary Queen of Scots considerable dramatic potential. The fate of Mary had first attracted him in 1782 (in March 1783 he spoke of having promised the publisher Weygand a play entitled *Maria Stuart*.) The subject matter fascinated him precisely because its treatment does not demand the large canvas of the expansive chronicling mode of *Wallenstein*. Schiller is determined not to get enmeshed in the labyrinth of historical and political facts; on 26 April 1799 he states in a letter to Goethe: 'Besonders scheint sich der Stoff zu der Euripidischen Methode, welche in der vollständigsten Darstellung des Zustandes besteht, zu qualifizieren, denn ich sehe eine Möglichkeit, den ganzen Gerichtsgang zugleich mit allem politischen auf die Seite zu bringen, und die Tragödie mit der Verurtheilung anzufangen' (NA XXX, p.45). It is Schiller's firm aim to poeticize the material as much as possible, to contain the turmoils of historical reality within the willed harmony of the aesthetic construct. He starts writing on 4 June 1799, yet despite the narrow focus of the play he takes some six weeks over Act I. He struggles to win the 'poetische Kampf mit dem historischen Stoff', despairing of his aim 'der Phantasie eine Freiheit über die Geschichte zu verschaffen' (NA XXX, p.73). The most obvious departures from historical fact concern of course the relative ages of the two queens, the dramatic meeting at Fotheringhay in

Act III, and the patterns of love and intrigue that involve both
queens and Mortimer and Leicester. By September 26th Schiller
is working on Act III, but, typically, the same impatience that he
had experienced with the *Wallenstein* material makes itself felt.
The constraints of the historical subject matter are too
oppressive and threaten to stifle the poetic impulse.
Exasperated, Schiller writes to Körner: 'Vor der Hand bin ich
aber die historischen Sujets überdrüssig, weil sie der Phantasie
gar zu sehr die Freiheit nehmen, und mit einer fast
unausrottbaren Prosaischen Trockenheit behaftet sind' (NA
XXX, p.98). He persists, however, and as particularly Acts III
and V demonstrate, the play increasingly succeeds in breaking
free from the shackles of historical truth. In June 1800 the play
is finished, and by July 1st Schiller has already started working
on *Die Jungfrau von Orleans,* a work whose very aim is to
triumph over the constraints of historical reality.

Maria Stuart stands out amongst Schiller's dramas by virtue
of its supreme formal control. On every level the play is marked
by that classical 'weise Ökonomie' which Schiller invokes for
example in his review of Bürger's poems: all elements are made
to serve the 'Schönheit der Form' (NA XXII, p.254). Action and
dialogue, the configuration of characters and the organization
of metaphorical and symbolic elements are all determined by the
aim to create an overall design of antithetical correspondences.
Such features reflect Schiller's renewed interest in French
Classicism and in particular his study of Greek tragedy since
1787. The tight formal control anticipates Schiller's
preoccupations with the austerity of ancient tragedy which so
dominate his letters of 1803, and the occasional changes within
the dominant iambic pentameter are experimental attempts to
approximate the metrical variety in Greek tragedy: '...man muß
das Publicum an alles gewöhnen' (NA XXX, p.95).

This strict formal economy by no means militates against
theatricality — on the contrary: the antithetical design is to a
large degree the very source of that theatrical power. Schiller's
aim had been 'daß in dieser Tragödie alles theatralisch seyn soll'
(NA XXX, p.85), and his hopes were fulfilled: the first
performance at the Weimar Court Theatre (14 June 1800) and

particularly the immensely successful performance by the Weimar ensemble in Lauchstädt (3 July 1800) prefigured the kind of popularity that the play has enjoyed ever since.[1] Critical opinion, however, was in many respects divided. On the one hand the formal achievement was praised: 'Groß ist die Kunst des Dichters in der Gruppirung und Gegeneinanderstellung der feindlichen und freundlichen Kräfte' (*6*, p.113). There is praise for the 'Schönheiten und Reizen der Poesie', the 'Reichthum und eine Fülle der Diktion', the 'schönen und herrlichen Jamben', and the fate of Maria is generally seen as profoundly moving. Her leave-taking in Act V 'ist so rührend und herzschmelzend dargestellt, daß gewiß wenig Zuschauer seyn werden, deren Augen sich nicht mit Thränen füllen' (*6*, pp.115-116). On the other hand, however, the fact that the play, despite its grand manner, is very close to the 18th century 'Rührstück' provokes objections. Critics doubt whether the play meets the criteria of classical 'Idealisierung' which, for Schiller, constitutes the very essence of poetry. The central task is 'das Individuelle und Lokale zum Allgemeinen zu erheben' (NA XXII, p.253). Thus a review of the first performance in Berlin (8 January 1801) argues that the enmity between the two queens may create 'rührende Situationen' and provide sufficient interest for an evening's entertainment, but that the subject matter is too narrow, bordering on the trivial: the workings of fate are reduced to the petty jealousy of Elisabeth, and therefore the play cannot adequately represent man's struggle against the 'gygantischen Schicksal' (*6*, p.122). By implication, the reviewer feels that Maria's particular fate is not truly transparent upon the universal 'Kraft des Menschen'. If this review implicitly charges *Maria Stuart* with hollowness, the Berlin writer Garlieb Merkel radicalizes these very objections. He is totally alienated

---

[1] The meeting of the two queens in III,4 and Mortimer's frenzy in III,6 met with some criticism: the language was felt to be too coarse. But the most controversial point proved to be the communion scene in V,7. The representation on stage of a sacred ritual was regarded as sacrilegious and Schiller was forced to rework the scene and cut the actual communion. In the theatre manuscript for the performances in Leipzig and Dresden, Melvil grants Maria provisional absolution in anticipation of his priesthood and the Pope's blessing.

by the play's grand manner, its increasing move toward the ritualistic. For Merkel, Maria's scenes in Act V are but a 'Prunkgemählde der Feierlichkeit', and his attack culminates in the observation that Maria's words and gestures are no more than a 'Reifrock des Prunks', that they are devoid of substance and constitute 'nur ein pathetisches Spiel mit dem — Fächer'. (*6*, p.127).

Such irreverence is hard to find in twentieth-century criticism. Admittedly, Merkel's polemical comments are echoed by Kraft (*8*) and Schlaffer (*13*), for whom the formal achievement, in particular the inherent trait of idealization, are highly suspect: for both these critics the play not only neglects, but fundamentally betrays the task of illuminating the historical-political dimension (*13*, pp.142-43). But such ideologically charged criticism is exceptional, and even Sautermeister, who sympathizes with Schlaffer's attempt to create a critical distance 'zu einem gefeierten Klassiker' (*11*, p.216), vehemently rejects the charges. The bulk of twentieth-century criticism may show some misgivings about the play's potentially rigid formal control, but generally displays almost boundless reverence in respect of its thematic import, the triumph of spiritual freedom over the constraints of fate. Essentially there are two schools of interpretation and both forge a close link between Schiller's moral-philosophical or aesthetic theory on the one hand and dramatic practice on the other. In the following we shall look at the central tenets of these interpretative models and touch on some of the problems which this present study hopes to pursue.

The Philosophical Reading and its Limits

On the most common reading, the play centres on Maria's development, her regenerative progression from a sensuous creature, a purely 'physisches Wesen' in the words of Schiller (NA XXX, p.61), to a triumphantly higher state in Act V. In terms of Schiller's theory, this higher state is either defined as the attainment of moral sublimity, 'Erhabenheit', which in the name of the moral law radically breaks free from the constraints of this world; or, more recently, it is seen as that supremely harmonious state in which the sensuous and the spiritual are reconciled. On this reading Maria goes to her death blessed with the grace of the 'schöne Seele'.

Let us first look at the model that focusses on the concept of the sublime. Such interpretations invoke in particular Schiller's essays *Ueber das Pathetische* and *Ueber das Erhabene*. In the latter we find the categorical Kantian statement: 'Der moralisch gebildete Mensch, und nur dieser, ist ganz frey' (NA XXI, p.39). And in *Ueber das Pathetische* Schiller ascribes to art, to tragedy specifically, the task of showing man's inherent potential for moral freedom, of portraying how human beings can, in the very grip of constraints, assert their spiritual independence: 'Der letzte Zweck der Kunst ist die Darstellung des Uebersinnlichen, und die tragische Kunst insbesondere bewerkstelligt dieses dadurch, daß sie uns die moralische Independenz von Naturgesetzen im Zustand des Affekts versinnlicht' (NA XX, p.196). The thinker and playwright in Schiller are at one in insisting that the moral triumph, transcendence, will only speak to us if we first witness the full extent of the tragic protagonist's suffering: '...der tragische Held muß sich erst als empfindendes Wesen bey uns legitimiert haben, ehe wir ihm als Vernunftwesen huldigen und an seine Seelenstärke glauben' (NA XX, p.196) and: 'Das erste Gesetz der tragischen Kunst war Darstellung der leidenden Natur. Das zweyte ist Darstellung des moralischen Widerstandes gegen das Leiden' (NA XX, p.199).

Schiller distinguishes between 'das Erhabene der Fassung' and 'das Erhabene der Handlung' (NA XX, p.211). The former is what we commonly call stoic dignity, in other words, a spiritual composure which remains unperturbed by the blows of fate. The latter designates a spiritual process: man either chooses suffering in the name of moral duty, or, having offended against moral duty, accepts suffering in expiation of that moral transgression. In accordance with these tenets, critics generally argue that in Acts I and III Maria is the unregenerate physical creature, suffering in her imprisonment and struggling to get out at any price. Her determination not to submit but to fight 'Macht mit Macht' (947) is indeed almost a literal translation of 'physische

Kultur' as defined in *Ueber das Erhabene,* that primitive state
'wenn der Mensch der Gewalt Gewalt entgegensetzt' (NA XXI,
p.39). By Act V, however, so the argument runs, Maria attains
that supreme state of the 'moralisch gebildete Mensch' (NA
XXI, p.39): she not only accepts her death with stoic dignity and
grace, but imposes her free moral will on the inevitable by
conceiving of it as atonement for her connivance at the murder
of Darnley:

> Gott würdigt mich, durch diesen unverdienten Tod
> Die frühe schwere Blutschuld abzubüßen. (3735ff.)

Again the critic can point to the overt links between theory and
practice: Kennedy's account (V, 1) that Maria, when faced with
the inevitable, was suddenly granted the strength to shed 'der
Erde Hoffnung' (3406) and 'glaubenvoll den Himmel zu
ergreifen' (3408) parallels Schiller's definition of the workings of
sublimity: 'Nicht allmählig (denn es gibt von der Abhängigkeit
keinen Uebergang zur Freyheit), sondern plötzlich und durch
eine Erschütterung, reißt es den selbständigen Geist aus dem
Netze los, womit die verfeinerte Sinnlichkeit ihn umstrickte'
(NA XXI, p.45). And Maria's stance in Act V is precisely
marked by that stoic attitude which *Ueber das Erhabene* defines
in moral terms as 'Resignation in die Nothwendigkeit' and in
religious terms as 'Ergebung in den göttlichen Rathschluß' (NA
XXI, p.40).

On this reading, then, the play centres on Maria's transformation from a physical creature into the free moral agent,
and it is this painful regenerative process which fills us with both
compassion and admiration. But this interpretation raises as
many problems as it solves. Critics cannot, for example, agree
on the exact point at which Maria's regeneration begins, and, as
a later chapter will show, I do not think that the question allows
a clear-cut answer. Furthermore, even if we grant that a sudden
and radical change takes place in Maria and view the function of
her religiosity as analogous with that of morality, we yet face the
problem of having to account·for all the 'Kostbarkeiten' and
'Reichtümer' that are being assembled by Maria's servants in

Act V, and we may well ask in the words of Kennedy:

> Und Eure Blicke fragen mich: was soll
> Das Prachtgerät in diesem Ort des Todes? (3456f.)

It is at this problematic point that the other school of interpretation sets in: in the wake of von Wiese's study, Graham and
Sautermeister shift the axis of the argument away from Kantian
dualism, the antagonism between sensuousness and morality,
and take instead as their operative category Schiller's synthesis
concept of 'das Schöne', the harmonious fusion of the physical
and the spiritual, of sensuous inclination ('Neigung') and moral
duty ('Pflicht'). On this reading, Maria is also imperfect up to
Act V, but on the threshold of death she attains that ideal
synthesis of sensuousness and morality, that wholeness which
obeys the dictates of 'Vernunft mit Freuden' (NA XX, p.283).
From this point of view, the splendour of Maria's costume and
all the precious objects are at one with the radiance of Maria's
moral state. They are sanctified, transsubstantiated, as are the
bread and wine in the communion, and Maria herself. As
Sautermeister writes: 'Äußerer Schmuck, sakraler Gestus,
religiöse Gegenstände und Riten verwandeln die Bühne in das
feierlich-festliche Symbol des göttlichen Zustands einer schönen
Seele' (*11*, p.198 and *12*, pp.212-14). In fully integrating the
physical and spiritual, such interpretations enact the kind of
synthesis that Maria herself invokes:

> ...Vergönnet mir noch einmal
> der Erde Glanz auf meinem Weg zum Himmel!
> (3548f.)

Yet again a number of problems arise. The question
of Maria's moral regeneration remains problematical.
Sautermeister, for example, follows Kennedy when he declares
apodictically that '"der süße Trieb des Lebens" kommt in dem
Augenblick zur Ruhe, da statt der erwarteten Befreier die
Verkünder ihrer Hinrichtung vor Maria erscheinen' (*11*, p.196).
He argues that Maria attains the state of a 'schöne Seele'

because she has fully acknowledged her physical self and has thus overcome it. It is surely questionable whether Maria's scenes in Act V allow of such an unambiguous reading. As Mainland, for example, has pointed out, even as late as V,7 Maria's moral self-scrutiny is limited (*9*, pp.80-83). There is indeed a disturbing disproportion between the ritual of the confession and communion and its substantive centre, and one may even go further than Mainland and ask whether Maria's last speech, her words to Leicester, are really marked by the tenor of 'eine geläuterte Sprache' and 'aggressionslose Verständigung' (*11*, p.196).

But quite apart from such specific objections, both interpretative models — the invocation of 'das Erhabene' on the one hand and 'das Schöne' on the other — strike me as problematic; for they essentially treat the play as hardly more than an allegorical illustration of Kantian and Schillerian concepts, thereby reducing the vitality of the text to an almost mechanical function. In consequence, the characters tend to be invested with a stable value which borders on the schematic. Thus Sautermeister, despite his probing socio-psychological analysis of the two queens, in the end categorically contrasts Elisabeth's 'perfekte Inhumanität' with Maria's 'vollkommene Humanität' (*11*, p.179). The reductivist danger inherent in a philosophical reading of the play is nicely highlighted by Otto Ludwig in the nineteenth century. He takes the opening of *Ueber das Pathetische* and then takes the argument *ad absurdum*: 'Die Regel bei Verfertigung einer Tragödie wäre also: die Komposition muß so eingerichtet werden, daß der Held eine große Fassungsszene erhält, zugleich aber, daß er vorher einmal Anlaß erhält, sich als ein Naturwesen auszuweisen, an dem dann die Fassung nicht den Gedanken aufkommen läßt, sie sei bloß Fühllosigkeit' (*6*, p.175).

Furthermore, Ludwig touches on an issue which commentaries on *Maria Stuart* generally ignore: the problematic status of the spoken word. With the exception of Mainland, critics tend to take Maria's words, particularly in Act V, as reliable indices of objective truth. By contrast, Ludwig focusses on that syndrome which Merkel calls the 'Reifrock des Prunks' and argues that rhetoric dominates so much that we cannot penetrate to the authentic self beneath the verbal display: 'Den Leuten ist mehr darum zu tun, ihre Rednerkunst zu zeigen, und ihre persönliche Würde zur Darstellung zu bringen, als dem Dichter, uns Menschen zu zeigen. Da ist überall Draperie und Attitüde, aber nirgends eine Spur von unbelauschter Natur' (6, p.171). Ludwig's comments are of course intended to highlight the shortcomings of Schiller when measured against Shakespeare. Nevertheless, he unwittingly raises issues of considerable importance. By pointing out the sheer self-consciousness of the characters, the 'Draperie und Attitüde', Ludwig's remarks remind us of the fact that Schiller knows of the problem of authenticity and pursues it with great urgency in many of his theoretical writings. One thinks above all of *Ueber Anmuth und Würde* where he is haunted by the question how and to what degree we can ever establish, beyond any doubt, that dignity and grace are indeed the constitutive attributes in a person. Schiller resorts here to the distinction between willed und unwilled utterances and argues: 'Daher wird man aus den Reden eines Menschen zwar abnehmen können, *für was er will gehalten seyn*, aber das, *was er wirklich ist*, muß man aus dem mimischen Vortrag seiner Worte und aus seinen Gebärden, also aus Bewegungen, *die er nicht will*, zu errathen suchen' (NA XX, p.268). But then Schiller considers that even facial expressions may be willed and thus deceptive; finally he concludes that man could be in total control of the 'mimische Spiegel seiner Seele', in which case 'ist dann auch alles Lüge' (NA XX, p.269). While positing the state of grace, Schiller argues himself into such a tight corner that his very formulation becomes precarious: 'Grazie hingegen muß jederzeit Natur, d.i. unwillkührlich seyn (wenigstens so scheinen), und das Subjekt selbst darf nie so aussehen, als wenn es um seine Anmuth wüßte' (NA XX, p.269). If the issue is even within the philosophical discourse bewilderingly difficult, we may well ask how the state of 'Anmuth' is to fare in a play, within the complex interaction of characters, and in particular on the stage, where the display of grace is of necessity a studied pose. Indeed, Schiller himself raises the question. In a footnote he asks himself how the actor is to attain grace, given that 'er sie nicht *erlernen* darf' (NA XX, p.270). Here Schiller has no answer other than to suggest that actors as private beings will have to mature into total humanity before they can represent grace on the stage. Clearly, by this criterion many plays would be condemned to a solitary existence on the bookshelf. And in the case of *Maria Stuart* the problem of authenticity is doubly compounded: a good deal of textual evidence points to a play within the play in the sense that the major characters, in particular Elisabeth and Maria, are conscious of being engaged in a political contest in which the handling of the 'mimische Spiegel' is crucially important. In other words, the display of 'Rednerkunst und persönliche Würde' to which Ludwig objects has centrally to do with the political and personal battle between the two queens and their respective camps.

Subsequent chapters will be concerned with the difficulties that beleaguer our attempts to establish authenticity within the politically charged context of the play; but it may be helpful at this stage to look at one particular aspect which encapsulates the issue in its full urgency. As we have seen, critics attribute in Act V a transcendent state to Maria, be that the state of 'das Erhabene' or that of the 'schöne Seele'. Clearly, the text is organized along such celebratory lines. The antithetical structuring here reaches its climax: Maria goes to her death in the whiteness of spiritual purity while Elisabeth is condemned to remain in the gloomy realm of her worldly power. Yet, alongside the clarity of this allegorical design, we find layers which relativize Maria's spiritual attainment in that they explicitly suggest that her stance is yet profoundly rooted in that political combat. Thus Kennedy assures Melvil:

> Seid ohne Furcht! Maria Stuart wird
> Als eine Königin und Heldin sterben. (3379f)

Maria herself is elated to find in Melvil a 'Zeuge' of her moral triumph, who will ensure '...daß mein Nachruhm doch nicht ganz/In meiner Feinde Händen ist...' (3499-3500). In terms of international politics, the power of the Vatican makes itself felt:

the Pope, who has issued a bull against Elisabeth, has personally blessed the sacramental bread and grants Maria the monarch's right to drink from the chalice (3653f. and 3750f.).

There is, then, even in these few examples the suggestion that Maria's commanding stance in Act V has as much to do with moral as with political concerns. Once we are alerted to the political dimension, we are surely challenged to reflect on the status of Maria as heroine and by extension on the question to what degree the political context impinges on the purity of the philosophical idea that is at stake. It is a daunting challenge; and in my view we can only meet it if we adopt a more differentiated interpretative model than the straightforward application of Schiller's philosophical concepts allows. We may yet retain the link between thinker and playwright, but we must shift the argumentative axis to that middle ground in Schiller's theoretical writing where we see him engaged in constant debates with himself and his propositions, where we find that energy which Wilkinson and Willoughby see as the very purpose of his *Aesthetic Education*: '...not to fix the mind, but to keep it moving. And to keep it moving by changing the viewpoint' (*20*, p.lvi). Wilkinson and Willoughby are at pains to stress that for 'all the closeness of its organization' the *Aesthetic Education* is 'not really a "closed" structure at all. The circle of the argument is open at point after point' (*20*, p.lix). I would like to argue that something similar and possibly more radical applies to *Maria Stuart*: by any standards, the play's organization is extremely tight and clearly stands in the service of the philosophical design. And yet there are persistent points of discontinuity, of friction, which resist that strict thematic and formal organization. These points are not unlike the footnotes in the *Aesthetic Education* of which Wilkinson and Willoughby write: 'They often function like windows opening on to a world of psychic reality which refuses to be confined within any system of thought. A world of swift-changing movement...' (*20*, p.lix). In *Maria Stuart* that swift-changing movement expresses itself as the unending interaction of pure idea and contingent world, the flux of authentic feeling and reasoning on the one hand and political calculations on the other. By embedding a philosophical design in a highly charged political framework, Schiller challenges us to observe, metaphorically speaking, the chemical reactions that occur when the absolute meets and interacts with the conditions of the phenomenal world, above all the relativizing forces of politics. These are the kinds of issues which this study will address.

2. History in the Metaphorical Mode

The stress on the historical-political dimension may seem rather surprising. Apart from Mainland, who focusses firmly on this issue (*9*, pp.66-71, see also *15*, pp.106-12), critics either tend to regard the political framework as mere background, or they criticize the play for its narrow focus. Thus Stahl, for example, states categorically: 'the political struggle lying behind the rivalry of the two queens is only the outer framework of the play: its main theme is the development of the heroine's character and her attainment of spiritual freedom' (*16*, p.107). By contrast, Sammons is acutely disappointed by the play precisely because 'in no other play of his are political considerations in the specific sense so prominent', but unfortunately 'the issues raised in the fabric of the historical setting are made to matter and yet not to matter at the same time' (*10*, p.166). For many critics *Maria Stuart* stands as a formal masterpiece (*7*, pp.51-53), but Schiller's aim 'den ganzen Gerichtsgang zugleich mit allem Politischen auf die Seite zu bringen' is felt to militate against the very essence of the analytical play which by his own definition consists in the 'vollständigsten Darstellung des Zustandes' (NA XXX, p.45). Perhaps such strictures ought to be viewed with caution. It may be misleading to orientate one's interpretation by reference to Schiller's determination to free himself from the constraints of the historical subject matter. The expression 'auf die Seite zu bringen' may make us concentrate all too exclusively on the displacement of the historical-political dimension when, instead, we should first examine whether the very means which seem to exclude the realm of politics paradoxically include it — and include it perhaps more powerfully than the realism of the traditional history play allows. I would like to argue that this is indeed the case in *Maria Stuart*. True, the play operates with a high degree of abstraction: the text aims at the 'strengste Bestimmtheit, auf die genaueste Absonderung, auf die höchste innere Nothwendigkeit' which Schiller defines as the attributes of the true artefact (NA XXI, p.13). As, for example, in Racine, the events leading up to, and surrounding, the drama on the stage are only present indirectly — in the form of references, reported scenes, recollections. But it seems to me that the grid of historical-political conditions gains in strength precisely by being internalized rather than being acted out. In the form of references, facts become part of the argument and by being constantly modified, reinterpreted in the major debates, they reflect that dynamism of politics whereby given facts are transformed into shaping agencies. In other words, precisely by replacing direct, mimetic representation by this indirect mode, Schiller enriches the text in two senses. Firstly, in so far as historical events are not enacted, but given to us through the medium of the dialogue, the textual stress shifts from fact to interpretation, from history to the very making of politics: events in their interpreted forms become powerful political functions in the play. Secondly, the strict formal economy, the distilling process of abstraction, allows for the creation of patternings whereby disparate factual references begin, within the overall textual web, to interact, to merge into motifs and acquire metaphorical force which extends beyond the discrete events to the very core of the Elizabethan Age. In this sense, the restricted mode of neo-classicism yields a potentially wider and sharper analysis than the broad canvass of the traditional historical play.

Let us look at Act I in this context. It is, of course, famous for the sheer economy with which the background to the dramatic action is sketched in. By means of dense recapitulations and reported scenes, we are within a minimal time span acquainted with the facts; but at the same time we experience, within the mercilessly clashing perspectives of the various speakers, the sheer irreconcilability of the political conflict. In many ways the debates between Kennedy and Maria on the one hand and Paulet and Burleigh on the other simply confirm and act out that age-old enmity between England and Scotland which is crystallized in the image of the river Tweed, the riverbed of hatred:

> Die Hand am Schwerte, schauen sie sich drohend
> Von beiden Ufern an, seit tausend Jahren. (818f.)

As we move through the exchanges between Paulet and Kennedy, Kennedy and Maria, Mortimer and Maria and finally Burleigh and Maria, we get more and more sucked into the tangle of European politics which, with the arrival of Mary Stuart in 1568, press in on England with ever increasing urgency. Even if we do not pick up every factual reference, we yet gain an overwhelming impression of conflict and threat. It is precisely by presenting events in their mediated, interpreted form that the text intensifies the vision of a tension-laden, darkening international situation in which opposing interpretations are pitted one against the other. Paulet and Burleigh voice that 'uneasiness, even fear, of Protestant England in face of foreign threats' of which the historian Elton speaks (*24*, p.321).

The meeting between the two queens in III,4 is of course a supreme example of Schiller's interconnecting skills: it is both intensely private and public. According to Wilhelm Grimm, Goethe likened the scene to a meeting of two 'Huren' reproaching each other with their 'Aventuren' (NA IX, p.371), and an as yet unidentified critic, anticipating Brecht's parody, defined it as the encounter of two quarrelsome 'Fischweiber' (*6*, p.118). Indeed the scene combines primitivity, uninhibited theatricality with a design that is yet transparent upon the general, the political stage of contemporary Europe. Elisabeth and Maria face each other as the embodiments of two cultural systems. The issues of legitimacy, of divine and natural law, the efforts of the Counter-Reformation all gain immense urgency in the exchanges between the two queens. And as Elisabeth and Maria watch each other while at the same time being watched by their respective followers, we sense behind their encounter the international political scene, the mutual prying of the rival powers. In this sense, III,4 anticipates IV,10 where Elisabeth in her bitter monologue speaks of being entrapped in a web of

constraints — 'Umgeben rings von Feinden' (3212). The meeting
between the two queens, pitting the claims of morality,
humaneness, against the brutal facts of power politics,
reinforces the import of the relentless exchanges between Maria
and Burleigh in I,7 which so highlight the insoluble conflict
between political and moral imperatives. Again we are reminded
of the historian's perspective: Elton makes the point that, within
that particular political constellation, English law was, had to
be, twisted: 'From the moment that Mary took refuge in
England she created a situation which could not be resolved in a
way that was both sensible and moral. And yet — the
martyrdom of the Queen of Scots remains to stain the record of
Elizabeth's reign.' (*24*, p.370).

But the finest achievement of Act I surely lies in the estab-
lishing of that organizational principle which so selects and
subtly distributes factual references that, within the overall
texture of the play, they acquire associative, metaphorical
potency and form conceptual presences which capture the
central mood and traits of that age. Subsequent sections will be
concerned with some of the key motifs, but it might be helpful at
this stage to look at some major examples.

In I,7 Maria denounces the vacillations of parliament since the
reign of Henry VIII:

> Ich sehe dieses edle Oberhaus,
> Gleich feil mit den erkäuflichen Gemeinen,
> Gesetze prägen und verrufen, Ehen
> Auflösen, binden, wie der Mächtige
> Gebietet, Englands Fürstentöchter heute
> Enterben, mit dem Bastardnamen schänden
> Und morgen sie zu Königinnen krönen.
> Ich sehe diese würdgen Peers mit schnell
> Vertauschter Überzeugung unter *vier*
> Regierungen den Glauben *viermal* ändern —
>
> (777-786)

Beyond their primary function of a vehement attack, these lines
generate the image of an England, which, in the wake of the

Henrician revolution, with its establishment of the supremacy and omnicompetence of parliamentary statute, is highly volatile, open in its very dynamism to the forces of chance. Maria's lines reverberate with that sense of the random which, for example, the historian Bindoff highlights when he writes of Mary Tudor: 'At first sight her reign appears to provide the most convincing proof that the fate of religion in Tudor England was the sport of chance, the chance which governed the succession to the throne and which now had placed upon it the most ardent Catholic in the country' (*23*, p.167). The idea of flux, the loss of binding laws and values, is sounded as early as I,6 when Mortimer shatters Maria's reliance on the divinity inherent in royalty and points to the executions of Anne Boleyn, Catherine Howard and Lady Jane Grey (615-17). Maria can only find words again 'nach einer Pause'. In this silence there vibrate not only Maria's personal considerations, but the mind of the age, so to speak, as it faces the modern era which is governed and constantly reshaped by a succession of parliamentary statutes.

If we now turn to the text as a whole we detect how the metaphorical potential inherent in the specific historical references is developed into a dominant motif. The specific link with politics is retained in various references to the fickleness of the people — one thinks of II,3 where public opinion is likened by Talbot to an 'unstet schwanke Rohr' (1341) or IV,11 where Elisabeth echoes his words:

> Die wankelmütge Menge,
> Die jeder Wind herumtreibt! Wehe dem,
> Der auf dies Rohr sich lehnet!...... (3260-62)

But at the same time the notion of instability is modulated into a much wider, existential dimension. In II,3 Talbot, pleading with Elisabeth, conjures up the vision of history, of time itself, unfolding in an endless chain of changes:

> England ist nicht die Welt, dein Parlament
> Nicht der Verein der menschlichen Geschlechter.
> Dies heutge England ist das künftge nicht,

> Wie's das vergangne nicht mehr ist — Wie sich
> Die Neigung anders wendet, also steigt
> Und fällt des *Urteils* wandelbare Woge. (1324-29)

In highlighting the historical-political world and all its value
systems as being subject to constant changeability, Talbot's
words link with that strand in the play which in quasi baroque
fashion sees the world *per se* as but a stage. It may be full of
alluring promises, but it is devoid of lasting substance, and its
actors and actresses are caught in the irredeemable laws of
transience, of earthly vanity. Strikingly enough, even within this
existential dimension the link with the political world is retained.
Thus, in Talbot's description of the French court where Maria
grew up, the baroque tenor in such phrases as 'eiteln
Weltgeräusche', 'der Laster Glanz', 'der Schönheit eitles Gut'
(1385-1395) encapsulates the morally shabby splendour of that
Renaissance court and at the same time expresses the hollowness
of life itself.

All this is of course crystallized in the fate of Maria, who has
experienced the full turn of the wheel of fortune, and Elisabeth
articulates that fearful sense of instability when she reads
Maria's letter:

> Was ist der Mensch! Was ist das Glück der Erde!
>   (1528)

As this line suggests, the notion of 'Glück' is integrally linked
with the motif of flux. Throughout the play, it is seen as no more
than the insubstantial product of the random constellation of
political circumstances. As Burleigh points out, in the eyes of
her Catholic opponents Elisabeth is

> Nur eine Räuberin des Throns, gekrönt
> Vom Glück!..... (1289f.)

Talbot may hail the Elizabethan Age as a period of stability and
consolidation, he may praise 'das Glück des Friedens' (1307f.),
but this 'Glück' is never free from the constraints of the political

world. It is Elisabeth who admits:

> Ich habe diese Insel lange glücklich
> Regiert, weil ich nur brauchte zu beglücken. (3162f.)

As the foregoing examples illustrate, Schiller exploits the very tightness of the neo-classical structure. Mere references gradually merge into metaphorical patterns, and the sense of fearful uncertainty that emerges is a trait which for the historian is central to that age: 'The excessive preoccupation of the Elizabethans with the order of the universe and the fixed degrees of men reflects...an awareness of the instability of their own day when society was being dragged from its moorings by new ideas, new worlds' (*24*, p.261).

Let us look at one other example: Schiller's handling of Maria's captivity finely illustrates that modulation of fact into metaphor with which this section is concerned. Within a very short span of time Act I lays out the factual ground: Maria, having refused to sign the Edinburgh treaty and thus to renounce her claims to the English throne, still harbours aspirations. She poses a persistent threat to Elisabeth and her realm. As Mortimer assures Leicester:

> Maria hat noch viel verborgne Freunde;
> Der Howard und der Percy edle Häuser (1918f.)

In I,7 Maria first rejects Burleigh's accusation that she is instigating plots throughout Europe, but then, as Mainland rightly stresses (*9*, p.80), in a striking change to the present tense she admits that her prison is a centre of political activity which, given the overriding power struggle, knows of no moral scruples:

> Ist mein Gewissen gegen diesen Staat
> Gebunden? Hab ich Pflichten gegen England?
> Ein heilig Zwangsrecht üb ich aus, da ich
> Aus diesen Banden strebe, Macht mit Macht
> Abwende, alle Staaten dieses Weltteils
> Zu meinem Schutz aufrühre und bewege. (944-49)

As these lines suggest, Act I is a model of efficient exposition —
the basic case is presented to us with utmost clarity:

> Denn nicht vom Rechte, von Gewalt allein
> Ist zwischen mir und Engelland die Rede. (957f.)

But Schiller, who so dreaded the constraints inherent in any
historical subject matter, the 'fast unausrottbaren Prosaischen
Trockenheit' (NA XXX, p.98), imposes a poetic organization
whereby the import of the merely factual information is
progressively widened. In the first instance, Maria's lines quoted
above, the lexical patterns of 'aufrühren' and 'bewegen' which
echo other instances such as 'erregen' (69), 'umstricken' (73) and
'aufregen' (934), articulate the mode and modality of Maria's
'Gewalt'. She is a latent irritant within the English system of
state and exerts her influence in the secrecy of the various centres
of power in England and abroad. The patterning links strikingly
back to the very beginning of the play: here the secrecy of
Maria's aspirations and of the modes which, in her captivity, she
is forced to adopt is finely crystallized in the motif of 'geheim'.
One thinks of the 'geheime Schätze' (7), 'Geheimnisse' (9) and
the stage direction concerning the 'geheimen Ressort' with its
'verborgnen Fach'. The secret treasures are not only emblematic
of Maria's latent sensuousness, but also powerful ciphers for her
political aspirations as encapsulated in the 'königliches
Stirnband' (18).

Furthermore, all these 'geheim' elements stand as concrete
correlatives to the elaborate network of past and present plots:
the conspiracies by Parry, Babington, Norfolk, the secret
missions from Reims of 'entschloßne Schwärmer/In allerlei
Gewand vermummt' (1275f.) and of course the plans of
Mortimer, whose hopes rest in part on the ranks of Maria's
'verborgne Freunde' (1918). But ultimately, the ramifications
extend to the play as a whole and capture the very modality that
mark national and international politics in that era. In the
course of Act II the motif of secrecy extends to Elisabeth.
Inescapably caught between the necessity of having Maria
executed and the grave dangers that this might entail both in

terms of internal and international politics, Elisabeth too sees secrecy as her only viable weapon. Thus she admits to Mortimer:

> Bei solchen Taten doppelter Gestalt
> Gibt's keinen Schutz als in der Dunkelheit. (1606f.)

Not only must Morimer kill Maria at night, but Elisabeth's gratitude must remain shrouded in the 'Flor der Nacht' (1628). And finally, beyond the figures of Maria and Elisabeth, we glimpse all the secret aspirations and dealings of the European powers. It is a measure of Schiller's structuring genius that the smallest textual or visual details ultimately link and illuminate the political modality of that age. It is a period of growing conflict, of civilized warfare, and with its patternings Schiller's play essentially anticipates the modern historian's point of view. Elton writes: 'Elizabeth, Philip, and Catherine de Médicis were all opposed to war but prepared to work against one another behind the scenes in a manner which would have precipitated war at almost any other period of history. These seventeen years are therefore filled with a mass of negotiations, changes of front, agreements made and broken, secret and barely traceable doings, through which it is difficult to thread one's way.' (*24*, p.295). There is in this context one dominant motif which extends from individual behaviour and transactions to the sphere of national and international politics: it is the motif of the spectacle.

The Spectacle of Politics

The spectacle, exerting the powerful persuasion of word and image, is of course an integral part of the timeless mechanisms of politics, but in particular it captures the manipulative flavour of that period which Elton so eloquently describes in his study.[2]

---

[2] Tellingly enough, in his essay *Geschichte der Unruhen in Frankreich, welche der Regierung Heinrichs IV vorangingen*, which deals with that particular period, Schiller uses to a striking degree the vocabulary of the stage. His account is shot through with such motifs as 'Rolle', 'Bühne', 'Beredsamkeit' and 'Schauspielerkunst'.

Within the span of the play, there are only two instances of overtly aggressive exercises of power: Pope Sixtus V renews the bull issued by Pius V in 1570. The bull declares Elisabeth's excommunication, instructs the Catholic faithful to remove her, and absolves all her subjects from their oath of allegiance. And in IV,10 we find the secular counterpart to the papal bull — in signing Maria's death-verdict, Elisabeth equally cancels out the divinity inherent in royalty. Apart from these two instances, the play illuminates a Europe whose great powers seek to assert themselves internally and externally by subtle manipulations. The studied display of the spectacle plays a central role in this. I,1 refers to the 'üppgen Hof der Mediceerin' (48), the court of Catherine de Médicis, who precisely sought to assert the regal authority of her three sons by political manœuvres and spectacular displays in the Tuilleries. In his *Geschichte der französischen Unruhen, welche der Regierung Heinrichs IV. vorangingen*, Schiller denounces the sordid disparity between outward and inner being in Catherine and her glorious yet decadent court: '...indem ihr alle sittlichen Tugenden fehlten, vereinigte sie alle Talente ihres Standes, alle Tugenden der Verhältnisse, alle Vorzüge des Geistes...aber sie entweihte alle, indem sie sie zu Werkzeugen dieses Charakters erniedrigte.' (*6*, pp.7-8). The initial reference is taken up and developed in II,2 when Elisabeth rather pointedly contrasts the 'prächtge Götterfeste' (1119), the 'Schönheitsgarten' (1127) of the French court with the modest spectacle that England offers to the French delegation:

> . . . . Ein gesittet fröhlich Volk,
> Das sich, sooft ich öffentlich mich zeige,
> Mit Segnungen um meine Sänfte drängt,
> Dies ist das Schauspiel, das ich fremden Augen
> Mit eingem Stolze zeigen kann... (1122-26)

From the start, then, the 'Schauspiel' emerges as deeply rooted in the manipulations of power politics. The English spectacle of a cheerful people blessing its sovereign may be somewhat more attractive than the 'Götterfeste' of the French court; but it is, of course, embedded in the Machiavellian tactics of the Tudor tradition, the politic wooing of the people. On the stage of politics we may hear of the 'gesittet fröhlich Volk', a Burleigh may argue that the voice of the people is 'die Stimme Gottes' (3068), but backstage, as it were, Elisabeth repeatedly denounces the people as 'Pöbel', a base, fickle crowd 'dem der Gaukler nur gefällt' (3195f.).

The motif of the spectacle emerges in its full force in I,6 with Mortimer's account of his stay in Rome. His story suggests at first sight a purely private experience, a decisive educative turning point: a mind brought up in stifling austerity, 'Der Puritaner dumpfe Predigtstuben' (414), encounters in Rome the glory of art and experiences profound spiritual liberation:

> ...und mein Gefängnis
> Sprang auf und frei auf einmal fühlte sich
> Der Geist, des Lebens schönen Tag begrüßend.
>
> (454-56)

Not surprisingly, Mortimer's account has been interpreted along the lines of the Schillerian concept of aesthetic education, the beauty of art in which matter and spirit, the physical and metaphysical, are harmoniously fused (*5*, p.167, p.369; *12*, pp.214-15). Such a reading, however, tends to play down, if not ignore, the fact that Mortimer's case has far more to do with confusion rather than fusion of the two realms (*1*, p.324; *3*, p.56). A later chapter will return to this issue; at this stage I am primarily concerned with the political dimension of this episode. As the overall context of Mortimer's account makes clear, his conversion is by no means a merely private event. In a political sense, the Vatican harnesses 'der Künste Macht' (430) in order to exert commanding representative authority, just as 'der Säulen Pracht und Siegesbogen' and 'des Kolosseums Herrlichkeit' (426f.) are emblems of the powerful Roman empire. In this sense, the 'heitre Wunderwelt' (429) of Rome is as politically implicated as the splendour of the French court. Overwhelmed by the beauty, Mortimer naively concludes: 'Denn nicht von dieser Welt sind diese Formen' (450) — he is blind to the fact that the Pope is precisely one of 'der Erde Könige' (447). His account may be totally unanalytical, yet for us, the audience, the political dimension emerges very clearly: Rome teems with 'edle Schotten' and 'Franzosen' (460f.) who duly lead Mortimer to the foremost champion of the Counter-Reformation, Cardinal Guise, who is Maria's uncle. Schiller carefully sustains here the motif of the powerful persuasion of word and image: it is the Cardinal's 'Suada' (485), 'seiner Rede Himmelskraft' (489) which bring about Mortimer's conversion. Subsequently, in the Jesuit centre of Reims, Bishop Rosse uses his 'herzerschütternde Beredsamkeit' (515f.) to persuade Mortimer of Maria's divine right to the English throne. And again the power of the image plays a crucial part: Mortimer is moved by a picture of Maria, 'Von rührend wundersamem Reiz' (504), the Bishop mytho-logizes the image, heightening Maria into the alluring figure of Helen of Troy — 'Die schönste aller Frauen, welche leben' (509) — and then proceeds to describe her martyrdom.

Mortimer's account poignantly illustrates how 'der Künste Macht' (430) and the powers of politics interlock. The opening of Act II develops this strand further. The allegorical 'Ritter-spiel' (1079) evoked in the reported scene of II,1 does not only serve as a touch of local colour, the customary entertainment honouring the arrival of the French delegation: it extends the implications of Mortimer's account further by providing the foreground to the sheer deceptiveness of the spectacle. For Kent it is 'das schönste Schauspiel', a supreme product of 'Geschmack' and 'edler Anstand' (1080-82). Yet we know that the allegorical splendour is utter sham. From Mortimer (I,6) we have already learnt that Graf Aubespine is actively engaged in the conspiracy to rescue Maria — his palace is the secret meeting place — and thus the polished celebration of Elisabeth's 'keusche Festung der Schönheit' (1083f.), her being beleaguered by love's desire, is thrown into utterly sordid relief.

The opening scenes, then, illuminate the stage of politics with devastating clarity: lustrous appearance may hide a murderous reality — the Church absolves in advance the agents who may kill Elisabeth, Aubespine's palace contains an arsenal of weapons (2688-90). The art of the spectacle is as suspect as the art of politics which, in the words of Graf Aubespine, 'mit Verträgen spielt' (2694). We are acutely reminded of the dual meaning inherent in the Greek term *skhema* which signifies both the perfect noble shape and mere pretence, deception as retained in the English verb 'to scheme'. The ramifications as regards our evaluation of *Maria Stuart* as an artefact are of course profound. If the spectacle is seen within the text as being integrally linked with political manipulation, if its substantiality is at the very least suspect, then the question arises what status we can ascribe to the perfect form of the play itself, its supreme 'Suada' of word and image.[3] Can we unreservedly argue that purity of form coincides with purity of idea, be that the idea of 'das Erhabene' or 'das Schöne'? Or should we heed the warnings of Staiger, who time and again asks if the authority and integrity of Schiller's philosophical concepts are not relativized by the dramatist's sheer delight in exercising his manipulative power over his audience? The concluding sections of this study will be concerned with this issue; at this stage I would like to turn to the function of the court setting.

Courtly Plays and Players

The court setting functions essentially as a micro-version of the international arena: the major characters enact concretely that tension-laden mood of European politics which pervades the text in the form of metaphorical patterns. Schiller here displays all the skills gained through long experience — above all in *Don Carlos* he had fully explored the dramatic and thematic potential of the court setting. He now relies on those same skills, but the much more restricted focus of *Maria Stuart* enables him to develop the metaphorical transparency of the material with

---

[3] Wilkinson and Willoughby make the point that although Schiller failed to make a verbal distinction, the fundamental difference between 'Schein' in the sense of aesthetic semblance on the one hand and 'Schein' in the sense of deception on the other is clearly established in his theoretical writing. Within the context of this play, I do not think that we can or should insist on such a clear-cut distinction. *Maria Stuart* is in many ways a spectacle about the problematic nature of the spectacle.

far greater sophistication. The very restrictions of the classical
economy are thus turned into a source of richness: behind the
specific situations and actions we constantly sense the temper
and workings of the era. Civilized warfare, using the rhetoric of
word and image as a manipulative instrument, becomes fully
visible in the studied moves and counter-moves of the
characters. Just as the political scene is one of uncertainty, of
calculation ranged against calculation, of alliances formed and
broken at the dictate of convenience and shrewdness, so the
court with all its plottings and counter-plottings is a slippery,
unpredictable stage. Paulet warns Mortimer: 'Es ist ein
schlüpfrig glatter Grund, auf den/Du dich begeben' (1664-65).
It is a view echoed by the desperate Davison in IV,11 when he
pleads with Elisabeth:

> Ich kenne nicht die Sprache
> Der Höfe und der Könige — in schlicht
> Einfacher Sitte bin ich aufgewachsen. (3315-17)

Given the treacherous properties of this stage, characters are
forced to move cautiously if they are not to lose their foothold.
It is a vital tactical skill which the tempestuous Mortimer
typically and blindly denounces. He taunts Leicester: 'Wie
kleine Schritte/Geht ein so großer Lord an diesem Hof!'
(1753f.). Yet, as we know, even 'kleine Schritte' are no
guarantee for success. Leicester, a master of this particular art,
is on the point of being displaced by the impending alliance with
France and laments:

> Heruntersteigen soll ich von der Bühne,
> Wo ich so lange als der Erste glänzte. (1798f.)

Elisabeth, manipulating Mortimer and Leicester, is in turn being
manipulated by them; and at the end of the play even Burleigh
will be banished.

The interlocking of the particular and general, whereby the
characters' concern to outmanœuvre one another mirrors the
rivalries of the international powers, emerges most clearly in the

motif of role-playing. Schiller handles it with supreme skill. 'Verstellung' and 'Täuschung' are key terms here. The motif is introduced as early as I,6: here Mortimer tells us that Cardinal Guise, before sending him on his mission to liberate Maria, taught him the art of role-playing — 'Und lehrt mich der Verstellung schwere Kunst' (545). Act II proceeds to develop the motif. In II,2 the grand entry of Elisabeth, her entourage and the French delegation is as hollow as the 'Ritterspiel' which precedes it. In II,4 Mortimer, when questioned by Elisabeth about his alleged conversion to Catholicism, pretends that it was only a pretence — 'Die Miene gab ich mir, ich leugn es nicht' (1498). And II,5 links almost literally back to I,6, to Cardinal Guise's instruction in 'der Verstellung schwere Kunst', when Elisabeth, having already fallen prey to Mortimer's deception, ironically enough praises his mastery of 'der Täuschung schwere Kunst' (1574). In a Machiavellian inversion of moral norms, Elisabeth defines the master of deception as the truly autonomous agent: 'der ist mündig vor der Zeit,/Und er verkürzt sich seine Prüfungsjahre.' (1575f.). It may be tempting to view this statement as a devastating indictment of Elisabeth's moral integrity, to read her words in terms of Mortimer's denunciation 'falsche, gleisnerische Königin' (1632) and to invoke Schiller's reference to 'meiner königlichen Heuchlerin', which, ever since he used the phrase in a letter to Goethe (NA XXX, p.75), has become a common label for Elisabeth. But if we follow this course we are in danger of ignoring the fact that Elisabeth's hypocrisy partakes of an all-pervading pattern of role-playing. The manipulative 'Rednerkunst', the 'Beredsamkeit' (2713, 2740) which Burleigh perceives in Leicester, and the 'zweierlei Gesichter' (1703) which Leicester and Mortimer detect in each other, feature not only in all the intrigues around Elisabeth and Maria, but also play a decisive role in the larger historical-political realm. Thus Burleigh praises the men who sat in judgment on Maria as exemplars of integrity, free from 'Fürstenfurcht' (744); but Maria counters:

> Mylord, ganz andere Rollen seh ich sie
> In den Geschichten dieses Landes spielen. (771-2)

Similarly, Maria may praise Cardinal Guise, the integrity 'des vielgeliebten, des erhabnen Mannes' (469); but Burleigh accuses him of teaching 'Königsmord' and the use of 'falschen Höllenwaffen' (1270-73). Indeed, Burleigh's denunciation is very reminiscent of Schiller's own evaluation of the Cardinal, who in his eyes 'seine Privatleidenschaften mit dem Schwert der Religion bewaffnete und die schwarzen Entwürfe seiner Ehrsucht mit diesem heiligen Schleier bedeckte' (*6*, p.14).

So all-pervasive is the mechanism of role-playing that the desperate cry of authenticity 'Weg mit der Verstellung!', first uttered by Paulet in II,7 (1679) and taken up by Mortimer in the subsequent scene when he confronts Leicester (1923), is doomed. Maria's challenge to Elisabeth 'Und was sie *ist*, das wage sie zu scheinen! (974) may strike one as impressive: Seidlin, for example, views Maria as being representative of 'man in his freedom, in the veracity of his being' and argues that her 'insistence on authenticity challenges the very matrix of politics' (*14*, p.46). Yet matters are surely more complex than this. As we shall see later, not only has Maria's authenticity in the past proved to be morally problematic and politically disastrous; but more importantly, it is highly debatable whether we may speak unreservedly of Maria as the agent and voice of authenticity. Certainly up to Act V she is closely related to the other major characters in that role-playing is an integral part of her behavioural and linguistic patterns. There is more than Puritan prejudice to Paulet's charge when he accuses her of hypocrisy: 'Den Christus in der Hand,/Die Hoffart und die Weltlust in dem Herzen' (142f.). As we have seen, Maria herself admits that beneath the appearance of stoic resignation she yet strives to incite foreign powers, 'alle Staaten dieses Weltteils' (948), against Elisabeth. In her captivity, Maria is both on the margin and at the very centre of politics. She has only a few weapons left, but these are precisely those which play such a crucial part in the politics of that era: the manipulative power of word and image. (In this sense, Maria's veil, its dual function of half revealing, half obscuring, is charged with metaphorical force.) Throughout Acts I and III, Maria displays all the skills of persuasion for which the historical Mary was famous. As early as I,6 she uses the combined power of word and image to persuade Leicester, instructing Mortimer: 'Bringt ihm dies Schreiben. Es enthält mein Bildnis' (674). It achieves its desired effect on Leicester: 'Es ist ihr Bild!' *(Küßt es und betrachtet es mit stummen Entzücken)* (1725-6). We are, of course, reminded of I,6 where Mortimer tells us how deeply influenced he was in Reims by Maria's 'Bildnis' (503ff.). Even Elisabeth is profoundly moved when she reads Maria's letter in II,4, confirming Burleigh's fear 'Zu groß ist ihre Macht auf die Gemüter' (991).

The motif of role-playing reaches its climax in III,4 when the two queens confront each other. Burleigh has argued throughout that 'King's face makes grace', that Elisabeth cannot order the execution once she has met Maria face to face. Behind his back, the meeting, long requested by Maria and secretly desired by Elisabeth, has finally been engineered by Leicester and Talbot. It is in this sense very much a play within a play: if, as previously argued, the court setting reflects the political stage at large, then the meeting between Elisabeth and Maria is the very nucleus in this mirroring process. In densest dramatic concentration it enacts the traits and mechanisms of the political arena, in particular the manipulation of word and image. Elisabeth enters the stage quite overtly as 'königliche Heuchlerin': drawn by sexual jealousy into a beauty contest, assured by Leicester of her 'Sieg der Schönheit' (2037), she pretends that she is motivated by generosity, the 'Trieb der Großmut' (2284). But we must not ignore the role-playing on the part of Maria. Immediately before the meeting, Paulet challenges her to make use now of her 'geschwinder Zunge' — 'Jetzt bringet Eure Worte an' (2159-60) — and Talbot instructs her briefly how best to persuade Elisabeth:

> Gehorcht der Zeit und dem Gesetz der Stunde!
> Sie ist die Mächtige — demütigt Euch! (2192f.)

He advises a discourse that is 'ehrerbietig', full of 'Gelassenheit' (2195), and gestures that are 'unterwürfig' (2217). The suddenness of the meeting has taken Maria totally by surprise; in her shock, she first claims that she cannot possibly humble herself before Elisabeth. But after the initial turmoil — 'ihre Gebärden drücken den heftigsten Kampf aus' — she does show a remarkable adaptability in her linguistic and gesticulatory behaviour: Elisabeth has expected to meet 'eine Tiefgebeugte', whereupon Maria, at once and with explicit deliberation, adopts the appropriate stance: 'ich will vor ihr mich niederwerfen' (2248) and 'sie fällt vor ihr nieder', pleading with Elisabeth to raise her 'von dem tiefen Fall' (2256). A few moments later Maria again expressly reflects on how best to appeal to Elisabeth, how she should 'Die Worte klüglich stellen', how to use 'meiner Rede Kraft' (2289ff.). Finally she 'nähert sich ihr zutraulich und mit schmeichelndem Ton' (2319). To this degree, then, Maria's discourse of humanity and humaneness is dictated by the 'Gesetz der Stunde' as advised by Talbot — in other words it is wellnigh impossible to distinguish here between the genuine voice of veracity of being (*14*, p.46) and the studied use of 'meiner Rede Kraft'. This is perhaps the chief reason why Maria's appeal to Elisabeth, her desperate insistence on humane communication is doomed to fail. One may of course argue that the meeting between the two queens founders because Elisabeth and Maria are as irreconcilably opposed to each other as 'Feur und Wasser' (2202). But we cannot simply ignore the political context and hold that Elisabeth, 'kalt und streng' (2279), betrays the essence of womanhood which Graham defines as 'for a woman to see is to be moved and melt' (*5*, p.161). Much more fundamentally, the meeting is doomed a priori: engineered and watched over by the respective parties, it is destined to remain in the grip of politic and political calculation. It cannot yield the ground of spontaneous individuality. Maria has learnt her lines, as it were, for a very long time:

> Ich habe darauf geharret — Jahre lang
> Mich drauf bereitet, alles hab ich mir
> Gesagt und ins Gedächtnis eingeschrieben,
> Wie ich sie rühren wollte und bewegen! (2177-80)

It is precisely because both queens are far too firmly cast in their respective roles and know that they are actors, being keenly watched, that no breakthrough into authenticity is possible — until, that is, the staged play collapses into the primitive authenticity of mutual hatred and contempt. Up to that point the scene is inevitably, even tragically, entrapped in the political realm where the principle of 'doppelter Gestalt' (1606), of 'zweierlei Gesichter' (1703) compromises the value of both word and gesture.

Significantly enough, it is not only the motif of 'Verstellung' which links the meeting between the queens to the political stage of the court and beyond that to the international arena. There is also the motif of anxious scrutiny. The fear of losing face and thus dominance pervades the play and is reflected in the numerous stage directions instructing the actors to observe one another closely. 'Forschend ansehen' (1496), 'ausforschend' (1610), 'scharf beobachtet' (1726) are among the key terms here. This scrutinising dominates in Act II where the intrigues and counter-intrigues around Maria are being formed, but it informs in equal measure the meeting between the two queens, and in IV,3 it highlights the intense rivalry between Leicester and Burleigh. After the disastrous meeting at Fortheringhay and the subsequent attack on Elisabeth's life, Leicester is more than ever aware of Burleigh's watchful eye and taunts him explicitly:

> Jetzt wird ein Inquisitionsgericht
> Eröffnet. Wort und Blicke werden abgewogen,
> Gedanken selber vor Gericht gestellt. (2707-09)

Even in V,8 when they come to attend to Maria's last wishes, the tension is still there: the stage direction reads 'Leicester bleibt ganz in der Entfernung stehen, ohne die Augen aufzuschlagen. Burleigh, der seine Fassung beobachtet, tritt zwischen ihn und die Königin.'

This brings us on to one last motif which, in the context of role-playing, is of central importance: it is the motif of 'Fassung'. Critics tell us, of course, a good deal about Maria's composure, particularly in Act V. It is generally seen in terms of a moral achievement, the dignity of stoic composure. Perhaps one should tread more carefully here and first examine to what extent, in this politically charged play, 'Fassung' functions as a tactical stance and response deriving from the demands of manœuvring, of keeping control.

The necessity to retain 'Fassung' is naturally most acute with those figures who are involved in the plots around Maria. In II,8 Leicester, after his secret conversation with Mortimer, is startled by Elisabeth's entry, but rapidly manages to check himself: 'Leicester *(faßt sich)*' (1947). A similar example of sheer tactical skill is to be found in IV,6 when Leicester is forced by Burleigh to read out the letter which Maria has sent him via Mortimer. He 'durchläuft den Brief, ohne die Fassung zu verändern', manages to remain 'ruhig', and with supreme improvisation he turns the indicting piece of evidence to his advantage, claiming that his contacts with Maria were intended 'Die Feindin zu erforschen, zu verderben' (2939).

Such instances of composure serving as a tactical means should make us reflect on Maria's mastery of 'Fassung'. It is all too tempting to read her outward dignity as a token of her moral integrity and to contrast it with the restless equivocations of Elisabeth. True, from the outset Maria exerts a commandingly calm stance: indeed her very first line starts with the phrase 'Faß dich!', and throughout Act I she is concerned to stress her composure. This stance may bespeak a measure of moral reflectivity — it is the anniversary of Darnley's murder and Maria's conscience is stirred: 'Er ists, den ich mit Buß und Fasten feire' (280); but at the same time her composure also partakes of the political power game. In I,6 Mortimer tells her how moved he is by her air of regal dignity, with its 'Sanftmut' and 'edlen Fassung' (563). Interestingly enough, an immediate textual link is established when, in response to the news of the verdict, Maria says 'mit Fassung': 'Auf solche Botschaft war ich/Schon längst gefaßt' (586f.). From such details there emerges the sense that Maria is aware of her own commanding presence — it is striking that in the extremely brief scene of I,3 Schiller carefully traces Maria's displeasure at Mortimer's lack of courtesy: she notes it 'mit Unwillen' and demands of Paulet that he should spare her 'den Anblick seiner rohen Sitten' (255). It is above all Burleigh who shrewdly diagnoses that Maria's composure is an effective political weapon:

> Dies stolze Herz
> Ist nicht zu brechen — Überraschte sie
> Der Urtelspruch? Saht Ihr sie eine Träne
> Vergießen? Ihre Farbe nur verändern? (976-99)

Burleigh knows all too well that Elisabeth's 'Zweifelmut' contrasts unfavourably with Maria's composure — 'unsre Furcht ists, was sie mutig macht' (982).

Intent on 'Fassung', Maria fears only one thing: the sudden and unexpected. This comes particularly to the fore in III,2 and III,3 when Maria learns to her total surprise that she is about to meet Elisabeth:

> O warum hat man mich nicht vorbereitet!
> Jetzt bin ich nicht darauf gefaßt, jetzt nicht. (2162f.)

Her wish to withdraw, 'daß ich mich fasse', cannot be granted, and in the subsequent scene she explicitly fears that lack of 'Fassung' entails the loss of rhetorical control: after years of preparation 'Vergessen plötzlich, ausgelöscht ist alles' (2181).

Insofar as these examples highlight 'Fassung' as a studied stance, they suggest at the very least the composite nature of composure, and thus challenge us to reflect critically on Act V where Maria's stoic dignity dominates the stage: is this stance of a fundamentally different nature? Has it truly moved from the political order to the moral order, or does it yet partake of the dictates of the political stage? It is again Burleigh who is aware of the political dimension:

> Sie trotzt uns — wird uns trotzen, Ritter Paulet,
> Bis an die Stufen des Schafotts... (975f.)

As we shall see, the distinction between the moral and political order is tantalizingly elusive. The overall text places the concept of 'Fassung' in a dialectically shifting light: composure does emerge at times as an achievement, the conquering of primitive

energies, which contrasts with the destructive state of 'außer sich
sein' — a state which Mortimer, Elisabeth and Maria experience
(see for example 2105, 2470ff., 3089). 'Fassung' may then potentially bespeak human dignity. Yet, as we have seen, it also
emerges as a calculating stance, rooted in considerations of self-
interest or political advantage. That we should never lose sight
of the sheer complexity of the issue is sharply borne out by a
striking textual fact: Maria's role opens with the imperative 'Faß
dich!', and it closes with its supreme enactment. But the final
stage direction for Elisabeth invokes the very same category —
'Sie bezwingt sich und steht mit ruhiger Fassung da'. The critical
question must surely be how the roles of the two queens in their
closing moments interrelate. We may simply argue in terms of
antithesis whereby Maria's spiritual serenity stands in contrast
with the merely political, worldly composure of Elisabeth's
'Fassung'. But, conversely, we may ask whether the final
statement of the play, the 'Fassung' of the political stage,
reflects back on to Maria's stance, highlighting that her dignity,
to a degree at least, also partakes of political motivation, the
self-stylization into a martyr figure. Perhaps we should
acknowledge that both strands reverberate in these parallels: at
the end of the play, Elisabeth bows yet again, as she has done
throughout, to political constraint, adopting that stance which is
so vital in the power game; but at the same time there is,
however faintly, a sense of dignity, of acceptance, as Elisabeth,
after all the turmoil of 'heftigste Unruhe', 'höchsten Spannung'
and 'höchsten Bewegung' (V,11, V,12), stands silently in the
inevitablility of her fate. Just as Maria in the very turmoil of
'Furcht und Hoffnung' (3388) can rise to face the crisis 'mit
ruhiger Hoheit' (3480), so Elisabeth — in the final inescapable
moment, bereft of all support — faces up, in truly solitary
Protestant fashion, to her own self.

The image of Elisabeth, broken, yet holding her own,
captures poignantly the sense of being entrapped in a world
which, politically and morally, cannot grant certainty, substantiality. The various characters accept or respond to this
condition in different ways and degrees; but essentially the two
queens encapsulate the general sense of imprisonment, the urge

to break out. Elisabeth, tired of the political stage, longs to return to the days of Woodstock, her youth —

> Wo ich, vom Tand der Erdengröße fern,
> Die Hoheit in mir selber fand — (3158f.)

— and Maria, whose physical captivity in many ways stands as a metaphor for that general sense of entrapment, shares Elisabeth's longing. In III,1 she rushes jubilantly into the park:

> Laß mich der neuen Freiheit genießen,
> Laß mich ein Kind sein, sei es mit! (2075f.)

It is this voice of freedom, arising beyond the calculated figurations of the political game, that I would like to discuss now.

3. Intimations of Authenticity and Freedom

Within the spectrum of the major characters one can perceive a clear patterning whereby the players on the political stage on occasion voice the desire to break free from the constraints of politic and political calculation. The one exception is of course Burleigh, who is totally at one with his office, the task to preserve the stability of the realm. No private self makes itself felt here — the figure of Burleigh is no more and no less than the voice of political necessity and practical imperatives. In this sense he is a forerunner of Büchner's Saint Just, that other disembodied voice of political principle. With this one exception, all the major characters recurrently display a latent or overt desire to transcend the situation in which they find themselves, to assert either their emotional, passionate selfhood or the claims of moral integrity. These two strands are poignantly reflected in Maria's jubilant greeting of nature, the realm of unrestrained freedom, and Elisabeth's longing for the days of her youth when, free from the constraints of practical necessity, she found moral substance — 'Hoheit' (3159) — in her private self. The relationship between these two transcendent urges is of course highly problematic. Ideally they should coincide in a harmonious synthesis whereby the vitality of the 'Kind' that Maria so cherishes (2076) would go hand in hand with the 'Hoheit' of the mature, reflective self. But, as for example the account of Maria's past (I,4) or the case of Mortimer illustrate, the assertion of sensuous energies inevitably threatens to stifle the moral self. Conversely, the agency of morality may simply not be compatible with the forces of practical reality: thus Talbot's hopes of a redeeming humanity are cruelly dashed in the meeting between the two queens.

As we shall see, Schiller traces the inherent conflict between man's emotional and reasoning energies with the kind of subtlety that marks the scrupulous moralist and psychologist. But even more pronounced is the stress on the political element and its determining grip on the workings of passion and morality. In most scenes we are not allowed to forget that language itself is so infiltrated by scheming that the specific gravity of meaning is at the very least open to question. Leicester, Elisabeth, Maria may use the language of the heart, speak of love and desire, but within the rhetorical assertion of authenticity there vibrates also the voice of calculation.[4] In Maria's love for Leicester there is the hopeful dependence on his 'mächtgen Arm' (2124); Elisabeth's lament that as the sovereign she cannot follow the dictates of her heart is at the same time an integral part of her manœuvring tactics. Similarly in the case of Leicester there is a private self beneath the public mask, but how much value can we attribute to his agonizings? In II,8 he may curse his ten years of subservience to Elisabeth, his 'Sklavendemut' (1784), yet one feels that his outburst is not so much directed against the lack of freedom as against the lack of success:

> Täuscht mich am Ziel der Preis! Ein andrer kommt,
> Die Frucht des teuren Werbens mir zu rauben.
>
> (1794f.)

It is surely doubtful whether we can credit Leicester's return to Maria even with the smallest measure of dignity as Sautermeister does — in his view there is, in all the self-interest, 'auch ein ästhetischer und ein ethischer Impuls' at work (*11*, p.180). Even in Leicester's monologue of V,10, where in self-loathing he partly faces up to his moral deficiency, the calculating energies of self-interest stir yet again. The figure of Leicester as the very epitome of opportunism engages our attention perhaps most by

---

[4] Schiller wrote to Goethe that Maria 'empfindet und erregt keine Zärtlichkeit, ihr Schicksal ist nur heftige Passionen zu erfahren und zu entzünden' (NA XXX, p.61). Even so, one feels that Maria is not filled with that absolute passion which, in respect of Racine's characters, Odette de Mourgues captures so finely in the phrase 'free from that dust of secondary considerations' (*Racine or the Triumph of Relevance* [Cambridge, University Press, 1967], p.40).

virtue of its metaphorical function: his opportunistic acrobatics, the horrifying discrepancy between rhetorical assertion and lack of substance remind us that, within the political setting, all language, even that of apparent authenticity, must be gauged most cautiously. Furthermore — and in particular — the firmly retained focus on the political dimension enables Schiller to trace the relativizations that necessarily occur when absolute values assert themselves within practical reality. Unconditional vitality and morality may be admirable forces, but within the grid of practicality they are bound to be but relativized functions. Here, Schiller exploits the spectrum of his characters: they are not so much individuated entities as components in finely balanced configurations which measure various, often contrasting modes of being against one another. For example: when gauged by the intensity of a Mortimer, the cold voice of state in Burleigh or the calculative figure of Leicester strike one as profoundly deficient; but conversely, their pragmatism throws Mortimer's unconditionality into critical relief. It is this constant interplay of perspectives which lends *Maria Stuart* immense depth and richness: the issue of authenticity forms the centre of a threefold drama — a drama which is, in equal measure, intensely philosophical, psychological and political.

Energies of Passion

The voice of vitalistic freedom, the 'frei' of the passionate self, rings out with greatest urgency in Maria's jubilation at the beginning of Act III. Here, at the very centre of the play, we hear the aria of total unrestraint, exuberance. Tieck and Ludwig objected to the stylistic break caused by the sudden appearance of anapaests —

> Eilende Wolken! Segler der Lüfte!
> Wer mit euch wanderte, mit euch schiffte! (2098f.)

In their strictly aesthetic judgment, Tieck and Ludwig over-looked the fact that the unreality of the 'lyrisches Ergüsse', the

'Pomphaftes, Opernartiges' (NA IX, p.372) is commensurate with
the problematic state of 'süßen Wahn' in which Maria here
determinedly indulges — 'Ich will mich frei und glücklich
träumen' (2089f.): her vision — as indeed the concept of vitalistic
freedom — is precariously poised between beauty and delusion.
The double-edged quality of passionate energy is epitomized in
Mortimer, who in utter subjectivity storms through all barriers
of constraint. Not surprisingly, Mortimer has fared badly at the
hands of most critics: he is generally seen as a 'Schwärmer', who
is as blind to practical imperatives as he is to moral considerations. He rushes headlong into his own death, and
additionally, and far more disturbingly, into a disastrous
confusion of the physical and metaphysical. In terms of the
mythological imagery which *Maria Stuart* invokes, Mortimer's
blurred vision perceives Maria as a blend of Helen of Troy (84)
and the Heavenly Queen. Sammons and Berman (*3*, pp.50-51) in
particular stress the degrading function of Mortimer's
sensitivity: the aesthetic and religious experience of Rome has
'emancipated only his sensual, lower self' (*10*, p.160). Mortimer
has fared considerably better at the hands of those critics who,
invoking the concept of wholeness of personality, see his Rome
experience as a prefiguration of that harmonious synthesis of
matter and spirit which Maria achieves in Act V (*5*, p.369); *12*,
pp.214-15). That Mortimer's role is crucial for our evaluation of
Maria in Act V is beyond doubt. We shall return to this issue in
the next chapter; at this point it is enough to note that the text
illuminates Mortimer's passionate energy with the same dialectically shifting light that informs Maria's jubilant 'süßen Wahn'
in III,1: the very eloquence of his Rome account — Storz likens
it to the 'Arie der Oper' and 'Kantilene' (*18*, p.182) — alerts us
to its analytical blindness. It is this blindness which in III,6
develops into the delusion of 'stillen Wahnsinns' and leads
Mortimer into the deadly trap of Leicester's treachery in IV,4.
But at the same time, his sheer intensity does raise him above the
constraints of 'Der Puritaner dumpfe Predigtstuben' (414) and,
more crucially, above the drearily compromised being of a
Leicester. In the end, Mortimer is able radically to part company
with Leicester: 'Auch nicht im Tode mag ich deinen Bund'

(2804); and the pathos of mere subjectivist vitalism — 'Ist Leben doch des Lebens höchstes Gut!' (2578) — is finally modulated into the morally charged stance — 'Das Leben ist das einzge Gut des Schlechten' (2805), which is so reminiscent of Lessing's *Emilia Galotti*: 'Dieses Leben ist alles, was die Lasterhaften haben' (V,7).

The links between Mortimer and Maria are overt indeed. The two figures share not only the fervour of religiosity, but also an intense cherishing of subjectivist freedom. There are direct textual correspondences in the two roles. Thus Mortimer's account of the sense of liberation he experienced in Rome —

>   ...und mein Gefängnis
> Sprang auf und frei auf einmal fühlte sich
> Der Geist, des Lebens schönen Tag begrüßend.
>
> (454-56)

prefigures III,1 where Maria rejoices in the park:

> Bin ich dem finstern Gefängnis entstiegen,
> Hält sie mich nicht mehr die traurige Gruft?
> Laß mich in vollen, in durstigen Zügen
> Trinken die freie, die himmlische Luft. (2079-82)

In its intensity, the language of both characters repeatedly soars off into the visual and visionary. This is particularly pronounced in Maria — one thinks for example of V,7 where she ecstatically greets the divine presence as embodied in Melvil's priesthood:

> Wie ein Unsterblicher auf goldnen Wolken
> Hirniederfährt, wie den Apostel einst
> Der Engel führte aus des Kerkers Banden,
> Ihn hält kein Riegel, keines Hüters Schwert,
> Er schreitet mächtig durch verschloßne Pforten,
> Und im Gefängnis steht er glänzend da (3657-62)

Above all, the figure of Maria is closely linked to that of Mortimer insofar as the transcendent urge of 'frei' paradoxically highlights the lack of freedom, the destructive forces, that it entails. The fervour of the 'süßen Wahn' in III,1 links back to the 'Wahnsinn blinder Liebesglut' (325) which, as Kennedy reminds us, dominated Maria in the past and brought with it a chain of practical and moral disasters: the stormy marriage to Darnley, the murder of her 'Liebling' Rizzio (318), Maria's love for Bothwell, the murderer of Darnley. And even Kennedy, who tends to mythologize Maria's worst excesses, ascribing them to the forces of 'böse Geister' (363), highlights the social and political dimensions of Maria's unrestrained subjectivity: her shameless passion for Bothwell went hand in hand with a shameless exercise of power, the disregard for the law and the people, when she let Bothwell carry the royal sword through the streets of Edinburgh and forced 'mit frechem Possenspiel' the judges to acquit him (352). The link between private self and the public domain is further developed by Burleigh: in his accusations, the flames of passion that are so much the hallmark of Maria's life are widened into the 'Flammen des Bürgerkrieges' (840-41) and 'Liebesfackel' (1282) threatening to set the realm on fire. And ultimately the motif of the flame connects with the religious passions of that age: Maria's vision of the gathered faithful — 'Da wird die Glut zur Flamme' (3612) — is associated with the many allusions to the fervour of Mary Tudor, the intense efforts of the Counter-Reformation in which the fiery Mortimer is so involved.

The characters of Mortimer and Maria — and the associative patterning that surrounds these two figures — illuminate clearly the inherent flaw of passionate energy, the destructive state of 'Außer sich sein' which Talbot warns against (2443, 3089). And it is precisely this fundamentally unreflective mode of being which Elisabeth so envies (*5*, pp.153-55); *11*, pp.182-85). Even if we allow for the fact that Elisabeth's language of the heart is often in the service of political calculation (II,9), Schiller clearly establishes a pattern of antithetical correspondences whereby the self-repression of the virgin queen with her unfailing service to 'strenge Königspflichten' (1984) is seen to generate a desire for that 'vollen Kelch der Freuden' (1977) from which Maria has so fully drunk — 'Die hat sich jegliches erlaubt' (1976). Entrapped in the role of the ruler, a web of demands and expectations, Elisabeth tries to create spaces of personal freedom by combining gestures of politic obliging with the discourse of non-obligation. Thus in her dealings with the French delegation, she refers to the 'vertraulich Band' (1223) as she decorates Bellievre with the blue ribbon. But it is the language of promise which is as yet not binding. Handing him the ring, she reminds him:

> Es ist
> *Noch* keine Kette, bindet mich noch nicht,
> Doch kann ein Reif draus werden, der mich bindet.
> (1212-14)

That such tactics necessarily entail debasing hypocrisy goes without saying. It emerges most overtly in Elisabeth's scene with Mortimer (II,6) where she holds out the promise of sexual love (1630f.). It is manipulative virginity at its worst — one thinks of Leicester's experience:

> Geliebkost jetzt von ihrer Zärtlichkeit
> Und jetzt mit sprödem Stolz zurückgestoßen (1786f.)

Yet beneath all her skilful performance the political actress in Elisabeth is tired of the stage, of being dependent on public applause, and longs to throw off the constraints of her role. Given the sheer weight of these constraints, it is inevitable that the one moment when the passionate self breaks out proves to be a catastrophic eruption: in III,4 the studied discourse finally collapses, both queens tear off their masks, yet the space of freedom and truthfulness thus created reveals but a horrifying primitivity. Once again, Schiller traces the issue of authenticity into its fullest ramifications. Maria's insistence on living free from 'falschen Schein' (2423), free from 'Bande' (2439), is thrown into critical relief. The eruptive ending of III,4 is both deeply liberating and depressing. In tearing off the veils of civilized behaviour, the 'Ehrenmantel' (2428), both queens debase themselves — just as in the past Maria, acting out her passions, throwing off the 'Schleier des Geheimnisses' (342), morally degraded herself. The triumph of primitivity reverberates in III,5 where Maria gloats over her 'Augenblick der Rache, des Triumphs' (2457), and it takes its final toll in IV,10 when Elisabeth acts upon the base dictates of revenge, signs 'mit einem raschen, festen Federzug', but then, typically, shrinks back in horror — 'tritt mit einem Ausdruck des Schreckens zurück'.

Within the overall context of the play, the freedom of passion is seen as profoundly double-edged. It may triumph over constraints, but in equal measure it may create the very conditions of lack of freedom. It would appear that the only viable liberation from inauthenticity is to be found through the agency of reason.

Energies of Reason

It is above all the figure of Talbot that points to the untainted realm of 'Vernunft' and opens up vistas of freedom beyond the compromised realm of political calculation. In speech after speech he appeals to the absolute norms of morality — 'denn die Hinrichtung/Der Stuart ist ein ungerechtes Mittel' (1316f.) — to Elisabeth's humanity — 'Der eignen Milde folge du getrost' (1342) and 'Dein Herz hat Gott gerührt,/Gehorche dieser himmlischen Bewegung!' (1543f.) — and to the practical wisdom of rulership:

> Sie wird
> Vom Grab erstehen, eine Zwietrachtsgöttin,
> Ein Rachegeist in deinem Reich herumgehn
> Und deines Volkes Herzen von dir wenden. (3117-20)

Taken as a whole, Talbot's arguments envisage an ideal synthesis in which morality, humanity and political prudence are fused. Yet how viable is this voice? In practical terms, his propositions would seem to be highly problematic. His arguments largely bypass the dangers to the state which Maria's captivity has proved to entail. His imperative 'Versuchs!' (1334)

disregards the political risk that Elisabeth would run if she refused to sign the verdict — Talbot simply assumes that the execution of Maria would make the people turn away in horror from Elisabeth. Furthermore, beneath the rhetorical weightiness of Talbot's pleading, the logic of his political reasoning emerges as disturbingly faulty. He repeatedly points out the fickleness of the people and the times —

> ...Wie sich
> Die Neigung anders wendet, also steigt
> Und fällt des *Urteils* wandelbare Woge. (1327-29)

and yet he argues that Elisabeth, in exercising her own free will, can shape public perception and opinion once and for all:

> Zeig denen, die dir anders raten wollen,
> Die Wahrheit deines königlichen Zorns,
> Schnell wirst du die Notwendigkeit verschwinden
> Und Recht in Unrecht sich verwandeln sehn.
> (1336-39)

In essence then Talbot insists both on the ruler's dependence on the people and the ruler's ultimate independence. He blurs the issue when on the one hand he refers to public opinion as a 'wandelbare Woge' and on the other hand asserts that Elisabeth has the power to turn that 'Woge' into firm stability. Talbot's pleadings with Elisabeth are attractive, impressive, but there is a perceptible discrepancy between verbal performance and argumentative substance. On close scrutiny, the voice of morality within the political system verges on bankruptcy. In this sense Talbot's parting words to Elisabeth in V,15

> ...Ich habe deinen edlern Teil
> Nicht retten können. Lebe, herrsche glücklich!
> (4027f.)

amount perhaps not so much to moral condemnation as to an acknowledgment that the moral order is fundamentally incompatible with the political order, that practical reality demands, for better or for worse, a more flexibly shaping hand:

> Und diese grade Hand, sie ist zu starr,
> Um deine neuen Taten zu versiegeln. (4023f.)

Talbot hands back the seal of his office, and there is more than the weariness of old age in this gesture. It is the exhaustion that can be felt as the ground bass in Elisabeth's voice throughout the play. It dominates at her very first entry, in her responses to the demands of the French delegation, and it is the opening note of the subsequent scene when, in response to Burleigh's eloquent evocation of her people's 'heißen Wünsche' (1246), Elisabeth laconically asks: 'Was wünscht mein Volk noch? Sprecht, Mylord' (1254). Of course the text highlights at regular intervals the manipulative moves of Elisabeth, but as the foregoing chapters have argued, we are also constantly reminded that Elisabeth is only one among many equally skilled players, that her performance is matched by those of France, Spain, the Vatican. Elisabeth is double-tongued in her political dealings, but at the very centre her voice is brutally and tragically clear. Her Machiavellian diagnosis

> Ihr kennt die Welt nicht, Ritter. Was man *scheint*
> Hat jedermann zum Richter, was man *ist*, hat keinen
> (1601f.)

may be profoundly unattractive, but it constitutes a fundamental political truth. In IV,10 Elisabeth traces the implications in merciless detail and frankness. She is alone on the stage and able to speak freely, and the energies of this freedom are channelled into the analysis of lack of freedom. The voice of authenticity is forced to articulate the principle of inauthenticity and places it at the heart of the political realm. The tight pattern of the modal verb 'müssen' which dominates Elisabeth's monologue encapsulates the all-pervasive web of constraints that informs her language throughout the play in such lexical clusters as 'sollen', 'dringen', 'drängen'. In II,2 Elisabeth

had diagnosed the lack of freedom of a woman who is subjected
to the mechanism of sexual politics, the imprisoning force of the
'Naturzweck',

> Der *eine* Hälfte des Geschlechts der Menschen
> Der andern unterwürfig macht — (1183f.).

Now she examines her role as ruler and concludes that here too
she is no more that a 'Gaukler', forced to please her people, to
'schmeicheln', 'buhlen', 'gefallen' (3192ff.). Morality itself is
closely scrutinised; justice is stripped of its claim as a virtue and
is instead defined as mere political necessity:

> Doch wars denn meine eigne freie Wahl
> Gerecht zu sein? Die allgewaltige
> Notwendigkeit, die auch das freie Wollen
> Der Könige zwingt, gebot mir diese Tugend.
>   (3208-11)

The disillusionment, the sheer knowingness in Elisabeth here
lends her surely the kind of tragic substance that we attribute to
Wallenstein, that other compelled and compulsive realist, and to
Büchner's Danton in the nineteenth century. With both figures
Elisabeth shares the horrendous experience that the freedom of
reflectivity, of reasoning, reinforces and increases the burden of
lack of freedom: 'freies Wollen' emerges as yet another
'Müssen' and fills the self with an overwhelming sense of
tiredness. Up to IV,9 we may ask whether Elisabeth's various
laments are genuine — one thinks for example of the lines

> Läg ich in meiner stillen Gruft! Fürwahr!
> Ich bin des Lebens und des Herrschens müd. (3144f.)

In the privacy of the subsequent monologue there can be no such
doubt:

> O Sklaverei des Volksdiensts! Schmähliche
> Knechtschaft — Wie bin ichs müde, diesem Götzen
> Zu schmeicheln, den mein Innerstes verachtet!
>   (3190-93)

Ultimately, one feels that Elisabeth is not only tired of her office and life, but of history itself: a subtle pattern pervades the text whereby the recurrent allusions to Mary Tudor, who like Elisabeth herself had at first been declared a bastard by Henry VIII, and the references to Woodstock where Mary Tudor, on coming to power, had kept Elisabeth prisoner on a charge of conspiracy, create an oppressive sense of sameness. In the words of the historian Neale: 'History was busy repeating itself, re-creating the setting of Queen Mary's reign, even to the imprisonment at Woodstock, Elizabeth now being in her sister's role, Mary Queen of Scots in hers.' (*25*, p.185).

Examination shows that the energies of passion and reason, which seem to enshrine the imperatives of honesty and truthfulness, are highly precarious, that at best they represent only fragile and relative values. Indeed, one could speak of a double tragedy here in that the very faculties which promise release from a fundamentally compromised world do not fulfil their promise, but are ultimately entrapped in that very reality. It is in this sense that, metaphorically speaking, Elisabeth's desire to retain her 'jungfräuliche Freiheit', her 'höchstes Gut' (1166f.) and Maria's longing to be a 'Kind' again are suffused with tragedy: the realm of the untainted is forfeited.[5]

Act V, of course, holds out the promise of redemption: Maria is granted the strength 'glaubenvoll den Himmel zu ergreifen' (3408) and goes to her death in the glory of both physical beauty and spiritual purity. One could argue then that in this transfiguration all the shabby figurations of the practical, political world are redeemed, that Maria atones not only for the sins of her own life, but for the base matter of the worldly realm itself. Within a Christian interpretation, redemption through the blood of Christ would ultimately extend even to the gloomy world of Westminster to which the closing scenes of the play return. But, given the enormous weight of Acts I to IV, with their emphasis

[5] The idyllic state which in Max and Thekla shimmers through the gloom of *Wallenstein* and returns as intimation in *Die Jungfrau von Orleans* and *Wilhelm Tell* is tragically banished here. In place of the harmonious interplay of reason and feeling we find the horrendous clash of III,4 which is but a violent extension of the psychic conflicts within Maria and Elisabeth.

on the political dimension, we find ourselves asking if the promise of Act V holds true, if the text unambiguously keeps its word.

4. The Promise of Redemption

As indicated in the introduction to this study, twentieth-century criticism is not beset by the kinds of doubts we find expressed by Schiller's contemporaries or the later nineteenth century. Ludwig could not forgive Schiller for idealizing Maria, for investing 'diese Furie mit einem Heiligenschein' (NA IX, p.384), and, as we have seen, for the critic Merkel Act V amounts to no more than 'ein pathetisches Spiel mit dem — Fächer' (6, p.127). By contrast, it is nowadays commonly held that Act V, in leaving the problematical, entangled world of Acts I to IV behind, constitutes the very climax of the play. Critics for whom Schiller's concept of the sublime is the operative category argue that in Act V a fundamentally changed Maria enters and that, in accepting her 'unverdienten Tod' (3735) as divinely ordained expiation for her involvement in Darnley's murder, she attains to that moral freedom which Schiller's theoretical writings pit against man's compromised world. On this reading, the sacramental transubstantiation vouchsafes symbolically the moral transubstantiation of Maria, her progression from a purely physical creature into a state of sublimity. Some critics, notably Graham and Sautermeister (5, p.170; 11, pp.195-97), argue in terms of a harmonious synthesis between matter and spirit and hold that Maria on the threshold of death fuses the sensuous and moral self and thus attains to the state of a 'schöne Seele'. Inherent in both these readings is a fundamental separation between Acts I to IV on the one hand and Act V on the other, and it is this fact which, I feel, leaves one with a sense of dissatisfaction. Of course, the contrast between the dreary world of the preceding acts and the solemn splendour of Act V is indisputable — Schiller pulls out all the theatrical stops to underscore Maria's stoic dignity. Yet if we separate these scenes totally from their overall context, and view them as a wholly

intact celebration of pure idea — be it the idea of the sublime or
'das Schöne' — the play's import is very much diminished. Any
such reading in fact implies that *Maria Stuart* in Act V parallels
the ending of Goethe's *Egmont* which Schiller had criticized as a
'Salto mortale in eine Opernwelt' — a questionable leap into
idealization which his production of the play attempted to
relativize. I would suggest that Schiller as playwright follows a
similarly critical course in *Maria Stuart*: in the end the splendour
of the scenes at Fotheringhay yields to the gloomy world of
political reality. Does this not suggest that the function of these
scenes is not only to wreak poetic justice on Elisabeth, but also
to remind us that while the dignity of Maria on the brink of
death may bespeak the glory of transcendence, it is yet
embedded in the political context?[6] To separate the block of
scenes from V,1 to V,9 from the rest of the play is to lose sight of
that subtle traffic of interconnections which link the worlds of
Fotheringhay and Westminster with the stage of European
politics, particularly as regards the motifs of the spectacle, the
power of word and image and the double-edged value of
'Fassung'. I would argue that the complexities raised by the
overall organization of the text can only come into their own
interpretative right if we retain the link between the spiritual and
the practical, political realm. For example: Wilkinson and
Willoughby hold that the protagonists in Schiller's later plays
overcome their compulsion — 'in taking up an attitude towards
it, they will become really free' (*22*, p.xlii). This certainly applies
to *Maria Stuart*: Maria's stance is commanding — but the text
also problematizes this 'taking up an attitude', thematizes it, as
we have seen, by tracing the political implications of willed
martyrdom. The critic is therefore challenged to acknowledge —
as the text does — that the transfigurative strand of V,1 to V,9

[6] The concluding scenes provoked considerable criticism at the time. They were
felt to be superfluous — A.W. Schlegel speaks of 'überflüssige Sorge, an der
Elisabeth nach Marias Tode poetische Gerechtigkeit auszuüben' (NA IX, p.381).
More interestingly for the modern reader, contemporary critics point out that
these scenes have an anticlimactic effect, tearing us down from heroic heights
and making us ask the prosaic questions of reality: 'Jezt erst, da uns der Dichter
in fortdauernde Verhältnisse, in die Welt zurückgeführt hat, jezt erst können wir
uns nicht der Frage erwehren: Und was nun weiter?' (*6*, p.129).

yet partakes of the figurations of the political world. In other words, even the wellnigh ritualistic mode of Act V is marked by that complexity within clarity which Wilkinson and Willoughby perceive as the dynamic centre of Schiller's *Aesthetic Education* and his creative work: 'Had not Kant, for the sake of a scrupulous definition, sacrificed the profound connexion of art with life? And was not a similar impoverishment implied in his definition of a pure moral act? An impoverishment of the concrete complexity of individual behaviour, with its mixture of motives, for the sake of a pure but unrealizable abstraction?' (*20*, p.xxv). In this sense I would argue that a critical reading of Maria's status in Act V lends the play greater philosophical depth, if by 'philosophical' we mean the tracing and retracing of the interaction between absolute idea and the conditions of concrete living.

It is Koopmann who alerts us to the fact that within all the assertions of established criticism there is a good deal of uncertainty, particularly as regards the most central element, namely the question of Maria's development from a purely physical creature to moral agent (*7*, pp.53-54). To pinpoint the moment of regeneration is fraught with difficulties — in consequence we find a bewildering spectrum of diagnoses. On Stahl's reading, Maria's purification has already set in at the start of the play; there is a momentary relapse into primitivity in III,4 when she triumphs over Elisabeth, but she 'soon regains her spiritual ascendancy' and in Act V she is 'in possession of das Erhabene der Fassung' (*16*, pp.112-13). But Stahl does not consider how we are to reconcile Maria's sublimity with the display of all the 'Kostbarkeiten' and 'Reichtümer' in V,1, her need to have 'Der Erde Glanz auf meinem Weg zum Himmel!' (3549); nor does he examine whether Maria's language in Act V is truly that of sublime composure. Benno von Wiese's thesis, that Maria's outburst in III,4 which seals her fate bespeaks 'ihren Willen zum Erhabenen' (*19*, p.245), is clearly highly problematic, and Beck's refined version, whereby in III,4 Maria both regains her spiritual dignity and yet returns to the state of a passionate physical creature (*2*, pp.185-87), has rightly been questioned by Koopmann (*7*, p.54). Sautermeister's argument that in Act V Maria attains to the state of a 'schöne Seele' (*11*, p.195-97) is in turn rejected by Sharpe: 'Maria is not, in fact, a "schöne Seele"' (*15*, p.124).

Of all the critics, Mainland is by far the most wary: he postpones the moment of moral transformation until the very end of the communion. The moment when Maria hesitates to accept the chalice encapsulates for Mainland 'the crisis in the inner, spiritual drama of Maria's life' (*9*, p.81). Yet even this cautious interpretation which stresses Maria's persistent feelings of hatred towards Elisabeth does not consider the problems posed by Maria's final speech to Leicester: the tenor here is surely not free from 'the longings and the remorse of earthly affection' (*9*, p.81). There is a sarcastic sting to her closing words which contrasts rather sharply with the assured serenity of such previous assertions as 'Ich fürchte keinen Rückfall' (3761). Such textual details suggest that there is no clear-cut turning-point in Maria's stance, that ambiguities persist to the very end. The built-in question marks make themselves particularly felt if one pursues Mainland's inquiry into the blind spots of Maria's consciousness and examines her responses in morally challenging situations. III,6 is a case in point. Here, Mortimer reveals his desperate rescue plan which will entail the deaths of all the guards and above all of his uncle, Paulet. Maria's rejection of Mortimer seems to constitute a firm step forward in her moral regeneration; yet closer examination reveals just how half-hearted Maria's response is. The gestures of rejection are there, dramatically and theatrically, so in the closing moment:

> Hier ist Gewalt und drinnen ist der Mord.
> *(Sie flieht dem Hause zu, Kennedy folgt)* (2597)

Yet beneath the rhetoric of horror, there is a disturbing lack of substantiality, of decisive resistance. As Gustav von Brinckmann commented sarcastically to Fritz Jakobi: 'Sie sagt eigentlich nichts als: "Nein, lassen Sie mich doch — was soll das — ich werde *schreien* — " (NA IX, p.382). There is indeed something hollow about Maria's protestations — so many are reduced to a monotonous sequence of exclamations. One thinks of 'O blutger Frevel!' (2522), 'O schrecklich, schrecklich!' (2524), 'O will kein Gott, kein Engel mich beschützen!' (2549), 'O welche Sprache muß ich hören! Sir!' (2564), 'O wer errettet mich von seiner Wut!' (2575). Such lines bespeak a lack of moral energy: there is a genteel note to Maria's protests which, coming on the heels of her violent outburst against Elisabeth, is disturbing. Take the lines

> O muß ich Hülfe rufen gegen den Mann,
> Der mein Erretter — (2581f.)

The sheer restraint of this formulation is surely problematic. It falls short of the intensity commensurate with genuine outrage at Mortimer's violent gestures — 'Er preßt sie heftig an sich' — and it leads one to wonder whether Maria exercizes self-restraint because she yet harbours hopes of being rescued by Mortimer. It is a point which reverberates in V,1 when we learn from Kennedy that even that night Maria hovered irresolutely

> Und zwischen Furcht und Hoffnung, zweifelhaft,
> Ob sie dem kecken Jüngling ihre Ehre
> Und fürstliche Person vertrauen dürfe,
> Erwartete die Königin den Morgen. (3388-91)

In V,6 Maria enters in full splendour, and the critical question must be whether this splendour that Merkel perceived as mere 'Reifrock des Prunks' (*6*, p.127) can yet be transmuted into the symbol, 'das feierlich-festliche Symbol des göttlichen Zustands einer schönen Seele' (*11*, p.198). Maria is 'weiß und festlich gekleidet' and this in combination with the *Agnus Dei*, the rosary and crucifix would seem to underwrite the profound change which, according to Kennedy, Maria has undergone. But, contextually, there is considerable evidence that this very change is yet rooted in the political power struggle, that the commanding stance is in part consciously cultivated. Just as Burleigh in I,8 predicted that Maria would proudly defy the English 'Bis an die Stufen des Schafotts' (976), so Kennedy now assures Melvil:

> Kein Merkmal bleicher Furcht, kein Wort der Klage
> Entehrte meine Königin — (3409f.),

that Maria will 'Als eine Königin und Heldin sterben' (3380).
Tellingly, in V,3 Burgoyn orders wine for Maria as he is
expressly concerned that she should not lose face, that her
enemies should not be able to claim 'Daß Furcht des Todes ihre
Wangen bleichte' (3452). Thus, when Maria enters, we should
bear in mind the element of (self-)stylization, the political
motivation within the stance of moral ascendancy. Emblems of
worldly power — her diadem and her 'großer schwarzer
Schleier', now folded back — interlink with emblems of
religious spirituality, — the *Agnus Dei*, the rosary and crucifix.
And the same process informs Maria's opening speech in V,6,
which is marked by a fascinating interplay of registers: it moves
from the code of religious certitude, the 'frohe Seele' (3483), to
the worldly regal assertion of 'einer freien großen Königin'
(3487), and then to the existential perspective, perceiving in
death the ultimate force which 'den Menschen adelt' (3491), but
it immediately returns to the tenor of self-assured royalty:

> Die Krone fühl ich wieder auf dem Haupt,
> Den würdgen Stolz in meiner edlen Seele! (3493f.)

There does seem to be a case here for aligning our interpretation
more closely than is usual with the historian's point of view
which holds that Mary deliberately stylized herself as a martyr
figure. This strand emerges from Maria's reaction when she sees
Melvil. She welcomes him as a 'Zeuge' who will witness her
'Triumph' and see to it that 'mein Nachruhm doch nicht
ganz/In meiner Feinde Händen ist' (3499f.).[7] The motif of the
spectacle comes particularly to the fore if we correlate Maria's

---

[7] That the concern with 'Nachruhm' undermines the morally free act of
accepting death is an issue which engages Janz's attention in his analysis of *Die
Braut von Messina* (R.-P. Janz, 'Antike und Moderne in Schillers *Braut von
Messina*', in *Unser Commercium, Goethes und Schillers Literaturpolitik*, ed.
W. Barner, E. Lämmert, N. Oellers, Veröffentlichungen der Deutschen Schiller-
gesellschaft, Vol.42, 1986, p.343.

joy at finding a 'Zeuge' in Melvil with her jubilation in III,5 that Leicester witnessed her triumph over Elisabeth: 'Er sah es, er bezeugte meinen Sieg!' and 'Er stand dabei, mich stärkte seine Nähe!' (2465, 2467). On a critical reading then Maria is here precariously poised between genuine spiritual grace and the studied stance that is yet rooted in personal and political calculations. A similar duality of illumination is at work when Maria takes leave from her servants. The scene takes us back to the beginnings of Schiller's career as a dramatist, to Lady Milford's last scene in *Kabale und Liebe* (IV,9). In *Maria Stuart* Schiller reworks the tableau of pathos, but by comparison with *Kabale und Liebe* he brings into the foreground much more critically the commingling of genuine ritual and self-stylization:

> Kommt alle!
> Kommt und empfangt mein letztes Lebwohl.
> *(Sie reicht ihre Hände hin, eins nach dem andern fällt*
> *ihr zu Füßen und küßt die dargebotne Hand unter*
> *heftigem Weinen)* (3567-68)

V,6 strives to enact 'das Feyerliche' as invoked at the end of *Ueber Anmuth und Würde* and employs the very means that Schiller mentions in the essay: 'Häufung vieler Anstalten...Verzögerung des Fortschritts...eine langsame gleichförmige Folge starker Töne' (NA XX, p.308). These tenets account for the principle of repetition: the motif of 'Lebt wohl', for example, is sounded six times and will recur in V,9. But at the same time, there is the persistent suggestion that Maria, whose 'Suada' is so acknowledged both by historians and by Schiller's play, is intent on staging her final and perfect spectacle. Tellingly, as she takes leave of her servants, the rhetorical composure finally breaks in the concluding stage direction: 'Sie wendet sich schnell von ihnen'. Similarly, in public she may assuredly assert that 'die frohe Seele sich/Auf Engelsflügeln schwingt zur ewgen Freiheit' (3483f.), that she feels 'Den würdgen Stolz in meiner edlen Seele!' (3494); it is only in the privacy with Melvil that Maria acknowledges the truth of her 'beklemmten Seele' (3584), which is not yet able 'sich frei und freudig zu erheben' (3585) because she has as yet 'den Heilgen nicht versöhnt' (3590).

Throughout V,6 then the celebration of the idea, of moral regeneration, is relativized by a disturbing note of self-celebration. It may be due to this precarious balance between authenticity and self-stylization that, as the *Schwäbischer Merkur* tells us, actors experience acute difficulties in trying to restrain their laughter in this scene (*6*, p.195). And it is clearly this kind of issue that Merkel must have had in mind when he so criticized 'Maria im Reifrocke des Prunks' (*6*, p.127). In our century it is Brecht who sharply develops the critical perspective. In his sketch *Maria Stuart*, the operatic element precisely aims to highlight the commingling of authenticity and studied pose: 'Letzter Akt...Während sie ihren seit Wochen einstudierten Abschied von den Mädchen nimmt mit einer leisen, etwas verschleierten Stimme — in der Musik ist, daß sie weinen sollen.'[8]

V,7 would seem to move determinedly beyond the reach of such corrosive doubts. The ritual of confession, absolution and communion stands as commanding objective correlative to Maria's spiritual transformation. The moment when she sinks devoutly to her knees before Melvil, the ordained priest — 'So lieg ich jetzt im Staub vor Euch' (3668) — would seem to spell a finally achieved humility, and Melvil's blessing speaks of all-embracing redemption: in death, Maria will find salvation — 'Blut kann versöhnen, was das Blut verbrach' (3739) — just as Christ's death atoned for the sins of man: 'Nimm hin das Blut, es ist für dich vergossen!' (3748). Yet Mainland's critical inquiry extends even to this sacrosanct scene. He argues that Maria, even in her confession, is blind to 'that habit of equivocation to which she is still subject' (*9*, p.80). In his view, Maria distinguishes falsely between the murder of Darnley at which she connived and 'the assassination of Elisabeth as a possible result of her plea for help among the foreign powers.' (*9*, p.82). Mainland's arguments considerably detract from the supreme status of those two lines which are generally seen to encapsulate Maria's sublimity, the workings of free moral will:

---

[8] Bertolt Brecht, *Gesammelte Werke*, Vol.15, Werkausgabe Edition Suhrkamp (Frankfurt, Suhrkamp, 1967), p.73.

>Gott würdigt mich, durch diesen unverdienten Tod
>Die frühe schwere Blutschuld abzubüßen. (3735f.)

I would agree with Mainland's line of argument, but find it difficult to accept his ultimate conclusion: in his view, it is in that silent moment when Maria hesitates to accept the chalice that she 'renounces that most noxious passion of hatred' and only 'in the moment of absolution, and not before, Maira is completely changed' (*9*, p.85). I am inclined to go further and argue that throughout the text there is something fundamentally incomplete about Maria's moral transformation, that, as regards Act V, there is a disjunction between religious ritual and moral insight which reverberates up to Maria's final exit. The role of Mortimer is a central case in point. Maria has chosen to accept her death as expiation for her involvement in the murder of Darnley, and in I,4 she defines her guilt, 'die schwere Schuld', as 'Ich wußte drum' (296, 292). Mortimer's plan to rescue Maria, as he tells her in III,6, involves bloodshed, the murder of his uncle and the guards. Once again, as far as Maria is concerned, it is a case of 'Ich wußte drum'. Yet she takes no action in III,6, makes no mention of it in her confession, and after her absolution her parting words to Paulet are as moving as they are profoundly evasive:

>Ich hab Euch schuldlos vieles Weh bereitet,
>Des Alters Stütze Euch geraubt — (3790f.)

Thus, in this final instance of a moral challenge, which in many ways gives her the clearest choice as it is free from the complexities of politics, Maria fails signally. As regards her relationship to Elisabeth, the issue is equally clouded. The register of purification is there in her 'schwesterlichen Gruß' (3782), regretting her violent outburst, and in her wish 'Gott erhalte sie/Und schenk ihr eine glückliche Regierung!' (3785f.). Mainland takes this 'clemency of her last message to Elisabeth' as a sign of her total change (*9*, p.85). Yet, does not Maria's final speech to Leicester largely cancel this clemency out again as she offsets her own 'zärtlich liebend Herz' against the 'stolzes'

of Elisabeth (3834f.)? Even here, at the very last moment, Maria
wields the power of self-projection. Her last speech, despite the
fact that it is 'sanft' in both voice and tenor, echoes her
rhetorical performance and victory over Elisabeth in III,4.
Leicester deserves of course to be annihilated, but in destroying
him Maria largely destroys her own status of sublime composure:
the force of her attack, underlined by a series of exclamation
marks, and the ill-disguised bitterness of such lines as

> Kniet zu den Füßen der Elisabeth!
> Mög Euer Lohn nicht Eure Strafe werden! (3836f.)

belie her assertion after the communion:

> Ich fürchte keinen Rückfall. Meinen Haß
> Und meine Liebe hab ich Gott geopfert. (3761-62)

To the very end we perceive that complex counterpoint which
informs the scenes V,1 to V,9. On the one hand, all manner of
theatrical and poetic elements serve to celebrate the solemnity of
Maria's moral regeneration. In the name of 'das Feyerliche',
Schiller exploits the principle of 'langsame gleichförmige Folge
starker Töne' (NA XX, p.308): the protracted leave-taking, the
leitmotif of 'Lebt wohl', the ritual of the communion, and
above all Maria's insistently recurrent assertions that she has
severed all links with the worldly realm, assertions which
culminate in the two phrases that bracket her final encounter
with Leicester: 'Nun hab ich nichts mehr/Auf dieser Welt —'
(3815f.) and 'Jetzt hab ich nichts mehr auf der Erden!' (3838).
On the other hand, there is a persistent sense of personally and
politically motivated self-stylization. In Benno von Wiese's
view, Schiller's play traces the outlines of a 'legendäre Heilsspiel' (*19*, p.239) — it is a reading which essentially takes
Kennedy's account of Maria's sudden transformation as
objective truth. Yet the actual text subsequent to Kennedy's
wellnigh programmatic announcement is surely more complex:
it constantly reminds us that to a very considerable degree it is
Maria herself who creates her own legend. Bereft of all worldly

power, she invokes divine forces as her allies and, more crucially, as glorifying agents. The fabric of her language is rich in motifs and images that parallel the splendour of all the precious objects and her dress: one thinks of such phrases as 'in meiner edeln Seele' (3494) and 'meine Großmut' (3554). As she is both the author and speaker of such passages, one senses that they have as much to do with moral ascendancy as with the will to exert a powerful regal presence. Thus Maria greets Melvil as 'ein Bote Gottes' (3640), hails his priesthood as a 'himmlisch Glück' ordained to bless her on the threshold of death (3656), and in a jubilant sequence of images and biblical references Maria stylizes herself into the divinely chosen vessel: just as, according to the *Acts of the Apostles, 5, 18-19* the angel of the Lord liberated the apostles from prison, so Melvil has conquered her prison, standing before her as a 'Himmelsbote,/Da jeder irdsche Retter mich getäuscht!' (3663f.). The link with III,1 where Maria dreams of Leicester acting as 'der Liebe tätge Hand', the 'mächtgen Arm' (2123f.) is as overt as it is disturbing: the same language that deludedly speaks of Leicester in religious terms —

> Bis ich das Antlitz dessen endlich schaue,
> Der mir die Bande löst auf immerdar (2127f.)

is now made to speak of the truly transcendent, the glorious power of 'des höchsten Gottes' (3666). The flexible capability of language is thus strained to breaking point. The profound issues which this raises will be discussed in the concluding section; in the present context I would simply stress that Schiller throughout the play situates the transcendent in a relativizing context, that he interlinks the moral and political, the physical and metaphysical.[9] Thereby he challenges us to partake of the dignity and beauty with which Maria goes to her death, but at

---

[9] On one level, the communion scene (as indeed Mortimer's account of his Rome experience) suggests that synthesis of matter and spirit which Schiller has in mind when, on 17 August 1795, he writes to Goethe that Christianity in its purest form is 'Darstellung *schöner* Sittlichkeit…und in diesem Sinne die einzige *aesthetische* Religion' (NA XXVIII, p.28); but on another level, given the critically

the same time, and in equal measure, to reflect on the relativity
of this move into transcendence. This process is most dramatically enacted at the end of V,9. Here Maria, at the very high
point of her leave-taking, implores Christ to receive her:

> ...Mein Heiland! Mein Erlöser!
> Wie du am Kreuz die Arme ausgespannt,
> So breite sie jetzt aus, mich zu empfangen. (3816-19)

But, in a bitterly ironic twist, she finds herself in the arms of
Leicester, the basest agent of reality: catching sight of Leicester
she is about to faint, 'da ergreift sie Graf Leicester und
empfängt sie in seinen Armen'. Suddenly, Maria's soaring
spiritual energies are brought into critically anticlimactic relief.

It is in this context that the role of Mortimer is of crucial
importance. The overall textual evidence shows that the
relationship between Mortimer and Maria is one of parallels
rather than opposition as Ayrault holds (*1*, p.324). As we have
seen, Mortimer fundamentally confuses the physical and metaphysical, the earthly and the heavenly Maria. In this sense he
prefigures Maria, in whose blurred vision the radically
incompatible figures of Leicester and Christ merge into one. In
the theatre manuscript for the performances in Leipzig and
Dresden, Schiller highlights this confusion with particular force:
in her final speech to Leicester Maria recapitulates the 'süßen
Wahn' of III,1. She speaks of the hopes which she had 'in süßen
Träumen gaukelnd vorgebildet' (NA IX, p.353), and as in III,1
Leicester is heightened into the figure of the all-powerful
saviour:

> ...ich seh ihn mitten
> In meinem Kerker stehen; alles ist
> Bereit zum Aufbruch, alle Pforten offen;
> Ich schreite endlich über diese Schwelle

---

illuminating link with Mortimer and the discrepancy between ritual and Maria's
inadequate moral scrutiny (*9*), the scene problematizes itself, acknowledges that,
in Storz's terms, 'Schiller sich seines lediglich ästhetischen Verhaltens zu den
religiösen Phänomenen weit klarer bewußt ist als etwa Tieck' (*18*, pp.183-84).

> An *seiner* Hand und hinter mir auf ewig
> Bleibt dieses traurige Gefängnis... (NA IX, p.353)

The parallel between the so easily deluded Mortimer and Maria exerts a drastically relativizing force which Graham briefly considers, but then dismisses by implication as an unthinkable possibility: 'If we condemn him for being unable to distinguish..., we are constrained to condemn Maria too for ending up in Leicester's arms after beseeching Christ to spread his arms to receive her in them' (5, p.369). I do not think that the parallels ask us to 'condemn' Maria, but rather to reflect critically on the precarious undertaking of grasping and asserting the metaphysical within physical reality, the absolute within our world of relativity. The sharply dissonant juxtaposition of 'Heiland' and Leicester, of transcendent idea and contingent reality, enriches the play both as a historical and philosophical drama: it captures the dual perspective which historians adopt when they view Mary's religious faith as both pure and yet implicated in political reality. And in philosophical terms, Schiller here — as throughout the play — raises those problems which haunt his theoretical writings.

At their most challenging, his essays are an unceasing interplay of absolute postulates and qualifying reflections. He never loses sight of the tensions between pure idea and practical world, and it is this which lends both his theory and plays a sense of intensely intellectual, yet human drama. If, for example, we ask to what extent Maria's act of grasping 'glaubenvoll den Himmel' (3408) is the free resolution of the moral agent and to what extent it may merely be a response *in extremis*, the flight back into the faith of her upbringing, we touch on a dual conception at the very centre of Schiller's philosophical writings: on the one hand, moral freedom is illuminated in its Kantian majestic glory — one thinks of such formulations as 'Möglichkeit eines absolut freyen Wollens' (NA XX, p.218), and the 'heiligen Reich der Gesetze' (NA XX, p.410); on the other hand, it is seen as a realm of last resort, as 'Flucht'. A footnote in *Ueber das Pathetische* views 'das Uebersinnliche' as the sphere where we, in extreme circumstances and bereft of any other resources, 'unsre Zuflucht nehmen müssen' (NA XX, p.205); man, faced with suffering, has 'keine andre Waffen als Ideen der Vernunft' (NA XX, p.202). Similarly, *Ueber das Erhabene* argues that constellations in life may be such that 'ihm nichts weiter übrig bleibt, als sich in die heilige Freyheit der Geister zu flüchten' (NA XXI, p.51). To take another example: if we question critically whether the Catholic faith and ritual in Act V can unambiguously stand as a symbol for the workings of reason (Staiger), we reformulate the misgivings expressed by Kant and Schiller: both recognize that, given human limitations, the invisible needs to be represented 'durch etwas Sichtbares (Sinnliches)'[10], yet both are aware of the danger that its representation may lead man fundamentally astray, that 'Fetischglaube' may take the place of the true 'Gottesdienst'.[11] Similarly, Schiller accords to religion and aesthetic taste the function of a necessary, yet problematic support. *Ueber den moralischen Nutzen ästhetischer Sitten* ends with the conclusion that ideally man should not need the 'Reize der Schönheit noch die Aussichten auf eine Unsterblichkeit', but, given our imperfect nature, the cultivation of virtue cannot dispense with the two 'starken Ankern der Religion und des Geschmacks' (NA XXI, p.37).

It is precisely the complex counterpoint of such questioning which reverberates beneath the firm surface of *Maria Stuart*. It is not surprising that these issues preoccupy twentieth-century writers as they return to Schiller's text. The least subtle reworking is Brecht's *Der Streit der Fischweiber*, which parodies the moral design by situating it firmly in the market place. It is perhaps Robert Walser who most poignantly captures that complex traffic which I have attempted to trace, that suspension between pure idea and contingent world, absolutizing and relativizing energies. A most deficient, yet deeply moving performance of *Maria Stuart* left him torn between rational reservation and sheer emotion, and he concludes on a note of profound ambivalence: 'Ich wußte nichts mehr, ich hatte genug,

---

[10] I. Kant, *Die Religion innerhalb der Grenzen der bloßen Vernunft* (Stuttgart, Reclam, 1974), p.256.

[11] ibid., pp.256-57.

ich packte das Bild mit meinen Augen, wie mit zwei wehrhaften Fäusten, an und trug es über die steinerne Wendeltreppe hinunter, zum Theater hinaus, an die kalte, winterliche madretscher Luft hinaus, unter den eisig-schauerlichen Sternenhimmel, in eine Kneipe von zweifelhafter Existenzberechtigung, um es zu ersäufen.'[12]

[12] Robert Walser, *Das Gesamtwerk* (Frankfurt, Suhrkamp, 1979), Vol.1, p.241.

5. The Dignity of Form

The objection may well be raised that the foregoing deliberations are far too academic, that the complexities discussed may arise in a close reading, but would surely be swept aside in the performance where the dramatic and theatrical power exerted by the sharply antithetical design of the play dominates. It is Staiger who speaks of Schiller as the Machiavellian master of the stage, who can manipulate the responses of the spectator — 'nach meinem Gefallen einem Ball gleich dem Himmel oder der Hölle zuwerfen' (*17*, p.251). Staiger is at pains to stress that we should retain our critical distance, particularly in respect of Maria, but he repeatedly admits that his own critical insights could not possibly withstand the magic spell of the theatrical spectacle. This is the reason why Staiger constantly alerts us to the 'unwiderstehliche Macht und ebenso das tief Fragwürdige' in Schiller's creativity (*17*, p.227).

Of course, the problems that Staiger articulates apply in varying degrees to most drama criticism: the text on the page and the play-in-performance are more likely than not two very different experiences. As regards *Maria Stuart*, Schiller makes precisely this point. On 16 August 1799 he writes to Goethe that he has incorporated a number of motifs 'die den nachdenkenden und instruierten Leser freuen können, die aber bei der Vorstellung, wo ohnehin der Gegenstand sinnlich dasteht, nicht nöthig und wegen historischer Unkenntniß des großen Haufens auch ohne Interesse sind' (NA XXX, p.85). Schiller clearly perceives the text on the page and the play-in-performance as two distinct entities, each with its own separate functions. As a text, *Maria Stuart* will appeal to reflectivity, scrutiny — as a play-in-perfomance, it will primarily speak to sensuousness. There is a detectable note of regret in his concession to the conditions of the stage and the audience; and the categorical distinction between reflectivity and sensuousness links with that large area in Schiller's theoretical work where he probes the status, the validity and limitation, of beauty. Some of his comments are particularly relevant in this context, given that it is precisely the formal perfection of *Maria Stuart* which so divides critics. It may totally sway the interpreter (see *5*, *11*, *12*,), but it may also be seen as bordering on the sterile (see *18*), even false (*8*, *13*), or, at the very least, in Staiger's view, as a serious impediment to analytical scrutiny (*17*, p.320).

Ueber die nothwendigen Grenzen beim Gebrauch schöner Formen takes up this latter point: 'An dem schönen Gegenstand erfahren wir nichts...Unser Wissen wird also durch Urtheile des Geschmacks nicht erweitert, und keine Erkenntniß, selbst nicht einmal von der Schönheit, wird durch die Empfindung der Schönheit erworben' (NA XXI, p.4). In rigorously dualistic fashion, Schiller goes on to separate beauty and truth, stressing that beauty and its contemplation are detrimental to probing reflectivity: 'Das Schöne thut seine Wirkung schon bey der bloßen Betrachtung, das Wahre will Studium...Durch die bloße Betrachtung wird aber nie etwas gewonnen. Wer etwas großes leisten will, muß tief eindringen, scharf unterscheiden, vielseitig verbinden und standhaft beharren' (NA XXI, pp.19-20). The essay presents some of those recurrent caveats that mark Schiller's deliberations on aesthetics. As regards *Maria Stuart*, Schlaffer and Kraft, one suspects, would argue that the play falls precisely into the trap that Schiller here defines so sharply: that the play parallels its eponymous heroine, that both are models of beauty, but fundamentally are deficient in, and resistant to, analytical scrutiny. Yet, given the overall orientation of Schiller's aesthetics, the stress on synthesis, on an art which engages all our faculties, we should surely seek to adopt an interpretative position situated midway between the activities of 'scharf unterscheiden, vielseitig verbinden' (NA XXI, pp.19-20) on the one hand and the contemplation of beauty on the other. In other words, we should bring to bear the analytical insight of the 'nachdenkenden und instruierten Leser' (NA XXX, p.85) on the sensuous experience which *Maria Stuart* affords. Indeed, the text itself challenges us to do so: a good deal of its formal organization, particularly in Act V, aims to compel us into a state where 'seeing is believing', but at the same time that state is also shown to be highly questionable (*3*, pp.50, 56). As we have seen, the play tells us how the political realm, its use of the manipulative spectacle, exploits the principle of 'seeing is believing'; and through the figure of Mortimer the text explores the philosophical dimension, tracing the disastrous confusion as Mortimer claims to perceive metaphysical essence in the physical images of this world.

As Staiger warns us, it may be difficult to resist the play's sensuous, theatrical pull, but I would argue that it is a highly rewarding challenge, that the play stands to gain in depth both as a historical-political and as a philosophical drama. Take the role of Maria in Act V: on first seeing the play, one may well be totally overwhelmed, falling into that state which Schiller so castigates as mere 'Ausleerungen des Thränensacks und eine wollüstige Erleichterung der Gefäße' (NA XX, p.199). But on a careful reading, the motifs of staging and self-staging may emerge, questions may make themselves felt and move us to ask, for example, to what degree personal and political rivalry still impinge on Maria's sublime composure. She will of course always hold the centre of our attention — this much is foreseen by Burleigh's statement 'Die Meinung hält es/Mit dem Unglücklichen' (1015f.) — but our pity and admiration will be tempered. Alongside the emotional involvement there will also vibrate the questionings and arguments that preoccupy Schiller in his essays. One thinks, for example, of *Ueber Anmuth und Würde* where he writes: 'aus dem schönen Vortrag einer Gesinnung oder Handlung wird man nie ihren moralischen Werth erfahren' (NA XX, p.283). Again the link between philosophical concerns and the subject matter of his play is overt, for Schiller's phrase reminds us sharply of the comment by the historian Pollard: 'The piety of Mary's death was no proof of her innocence towards Elizabeth, and the strength of her religious convictions was no guarantee for the morality of her conduct' (*26*, p.399).

Ultimately of course our questioning will not only concern the figure of Maria, but also, and more crucially, the status of the play, the act of representation itself. On a critical reading, *Maria*

Stuart moves towards that middle ground in Schiller's theoretical writings where he unceasingly reflects on the problematic nature of beauty, the precarious interconnection between sensuousness and morality. *Ueber Anmuth und Würde* holds that while the metaphysical, the 'moralische Kraft im Menschen' cannot be represented, it can be conveyed indirectly through the mediation of 'sinnliche Zeichen' (NA XX, p.294). But, as the essay *Ueber die nothwendigen Grenzen beim Gebrauch schöner Formen* suggests and as Wilkinson and Willoughby so eloquently demonstrate, Schiller's assertions unfailingly contain their own 'built-in warning system' (*20*, p.lxxx), precisely because all human endeavour is 'even at its best — profoundly ambiguous' (*20*, p.lxxx). If then the deliberations of the 'nachdenkenden und instruierten Leser' bring a tinge of ambiguity into the splendour of *Maria Stuart*, the play may indeed speak to us more urgently, illuminating those hardly decipherable areas in us where the noumenal and the contingent, moral urges and practical, psychological needs are tantalizingly interconnected. And the play as a whole will modulate from the monolithic assurance of the 'legendäre Heilsspiel' (*19*, p.239) to a recognizably modern drama that is concerned with and thematizes the problem of knowing and representing the metaphysical realm. It is in this sense that the closing scenes of the play are so moving: Maria's 'Rückfall' when she finds herself in the arms of Leicester rather than of 'Heiland' parallels the 'Rückfall' of the text itself as it returns to the compromised realm of Westminster. Both Schiller's protagonist and text are made to acknowledge the tangled human reality from which they spring.

Clarity of Form

Without doubt, *Maria Stuart* displays a clarity of design which is unequalled by Schiller's other plays. A good deal of this formal control is in the service of a play that is not only about a trial, but turns itself into a trial which invites us as readers and spectators to sit in ultimate judgment on Elisabeth and Maria.

The word-cluster of 'richten', 'Richter', 'Recht', 'Gerechtigkeit' and related terms pervades almost every page of the text and thus constitutes a lexical and conceptual axis. In this sense, *Maria Stuart* follows the lines of *Die Schaubühne als eine moralische Anstalt betrachtet*, which views the stage as an alternative court of justice that takes over at precisely the point where 'das Gebiet der weltlichen Gesetze sich endigt'.[13] Schiller made of course the point that his 'Maria wird keine weiche Stimmung erregen…Sie empfindet und erregt keine Zärtlichkeit' (NA XXX, p.61). This comment suggests a considerable measure of objectivity. But on the theatrical level, the sharp contrasts between the two queens — Maria's beauty, her vibrant being, versus the relative plainness and self-suppression of Elisabeth — and above all the contrastive design of Act V, clearly conspire to make us side with Maria. The structural principle of antithesis pervades every layer of the text. The fates of the two queens take their course in diagonal opposition: Maria rises from abject imprisonment and suffering to the resplendent glory of moral strength, whereas Elisabeth, the powerful monarch, gradually loses in stature and stands at the end morally indicted and isolated. The meeting of the two queens in III,4 is of course the central point of intersection. Antithesis also informs the act sequence, its regular alternation between Fotheringhay and Westminster. Act III would seem to break out of this determining chain: the park setting — 'Vorn mit Bäumen besetzt, hinten eine weite Aussicht' — holds the promise of nature, the realm of freedom, but, as we know, in the formidable clash between the two queens the worlds of Westminster, Fotheringhay and the Continental powers assert themselves with a vengeance.

Antithesis further determines the spectrum of the characters. As though on a chess board, Schiller sets them up in opposing, yet corresponding configurations. As Graham reminds us, each queen embodies those traits that are suppressed in the other: 'The Scottish Queen in her prison is as it were a part-image of

---

[13] F. Schiller, *Vom Pathetischen und Erhabenen. Ausgewählte Schriften zur Dramentheorie* (Stuttgart, Reclam, 1984), p.4.

her rival's clandestine eroticism, blown-up to full-size dimensions and candidly projected onto a vast screen...And so, too, conversely: in the figure of Elisabeth the poet has embodied, and enlarged, those constraining forces of conscience which in Maria herself have remained rudimentary, condemned to linger beneath the threshold of her consciousness.' (5, p.155).

Finally, the merest glance at the textual organization shows how painstakingly Schiller weaves dense patterns of correspondences and contrasts which interpretation must take into account. The foregoing sections have considered some of these. In respect of Maria's development one should also bear in mind the motif of the 'Kelch'. In II,9 Elisabeth, envying Maria for her unrestrained mode of living, comments bitterly 'sie hat/Den vollen Kelch der Freuden ausgetrunken' (1976f.), and Leicester responds: 'Jetzt trinkt sie auch den bittern Kelch des Leidens.' (1978). The motif culminates in V,7, in the chalice of the communion. As Maria drinks from the chalice, the earthly 'Kelch' of both joy and suffering is, perhaps, cancelled out. In close parallel there is the motif of blood. Maria will expiate her 'Blutschuld' (3736) on the 'Blutgerüste' (3734), blessed and secure in the crowning redemption of Christ's blood: 'Nimm hin das Blut, es ist für dich vergossen!' (3748). And for those who trust the symbolic force of verbal patterns Maria's death may even stand in expiation for 'Der spanischen Maria blutge Zeiten' (102) which are repeatedly invoked.

Schiller's grip on the text is tight throughout, perhaps most overtly so as regards colour symbolism. In Acts I to IV, the black of Maria's costume stands in sharp contrast to the colours of the court; in Act V her white costume, the black veil now folded back, signifies Maria's passing beyond suffering, the constraints of fate, as crystallized in the black of the scaffold and her servants' 'Trauerkleider', and in addition it denotes the triumph over the dark realm of worldly politics, the 'Flor der Nacht' (1628).

All such traits contribute towards that emphatic clarity in the play which either alienates or persuades the critic. Thus Storz, who so illuminatingly traces the antithetical relationship of cause of effect whereby every attempt to save Maria brings her closer to death (*18*, pp.172-74), feels that this outstanding formal control is a strait-jacket which prevents Schiller from developing fully the tragic potential inherent in the situations of the two queens (*18*, p.177). Kraft and Schlaffer's onslaughts on the play's idealizing energies are but vehement extensions of such reservations. By contrast, Sautermeister's study shows how persuasive the rhetorical and scenic power of *Maria Stuart* can prove even in the late twentieth century. In his discussion of Act V, the sharply analytical tenor of this largely socio-psychological enquiry yields to one of unrestrained eulogy: 'Maria hebt die Differenz zwischen äußerer Vollkommenheit und menschlicher Unvollkommenheit in ihrer Todesstunde auf. Sie wird zur schönen Seele: jetzt wetteifern die königliche Schönheit ihrer Gestalt und der Adel ihrer Menschlichkeit harmonisch miteinander' (*11*, p.195).

It would appear then that the critic who does not reject the formal mastery of the play outright finds it very difficult to resist the power of *Maria Stuart* — a power which is so akin to that of opera, urging us to suspend our critical faculties. Tellingly enough, in the nineteenth century the Italian actress Adelaide Ristori playing the title role scored enormous success in America, despite the fact that, surrounded by an English-speaking cast, she spoke her part in Italian! (*6*, p.150). Schiller cherished opera precisely for its powerful persuasion, arguing that the combination of music and 'freie harmonische Reizung der Sinnlichkeit' would contribute towards a higher spiritual receptivity — 'zu einer schönern Empfängnis' (NA XXIX, p.179).[14] But here is the rub: how can Schiller be sure that opera, or in this case *Maria Stuart*, may not simply produce sensuous indulgence, 'die schmelzenden Affekte, die bloß zärtlichen Rührungen' which he castigates in *Ueber das Pathetische*: 'der Geist geht leer aus, und die edlere Kraft im Menschen wird ganz und gar nicht dadurch gestärkt' (NA XX, p.199)? It is surely at this critical point that the activities of the critical reader must set in and, taking their cue from pointers within the text, probingly

[14] Letter to Goethe, 29 December 1797. On this point see Staiger (*17*, p.389).

reflect on the formal splendour of the play.

Ambiguity of Form

Let us in this context look once more at the role of rhetoric. On a first encounter in the theatre, its sheer power may overwhelm us. But in the act of reading, the persistent motif of 'Suada' will surely make itself felt and begin to modify our perception. References to Burleigh's 'Gewalt des Mundes' (762), Maria's 'Macht auf die Gemüter' (991), Anjou's 'des Schmeichelns Künste' (1804), Leicester's 'Rednerkunst' and 'Beredsamkeit' (2713, 2740) inevitably throw the spoken word into critical relief. They alert us to the questionable language of the various characters and ultimately conspire to make Schiller's own rhetoric problematize itself. In other words: if the fiery assertions of Mortimer betray increasingly blindness, ethical and religious disorientation, if the words of a Leicester devalue themselves in the very act of speaking, if the dignity of Maria's language even in Act V is felt to lack substantiality (*9*, pp.80-83), then surely the overall rhetoric employed by Schiller begins to acknowledge its own relativity, its precarious function in the service of 'that highly ambiguous and illusive phenomenon, beauty' (*20*, p.328). We are alerted to the fact that dignity of form is no guarantee of substance. That form is indifferent to the substance which it shapes emerges most strikingly if we examine Schiller's handling of rhyme, that epitome of linguistic-poetic 'Fassung'. There is a striking ambivalence at work. On one level, rhyme is used in traditional manner as a means of emphasis — one thinks for example of the conclusion to I,7 where Maria challenges Elisabeth:

> Sie geb es auf, mit des Verbrechens Früchten
> Den heilgen Schein der Tugend zu vereinen,
> Und was sie *ist*, das wage sie zu scheinen! (972-74)

Rhymes can serve as guarantors of substance. Thus Paulet in I,8 refuses to be corrupted by Burleigh and connive at a secret murder of Maria:

> Jetzt ist sie zur Bewahrung mir vertraut,
> Und seid gewiß, ich werde sie bewahren,
> Daß sie nichts Böses tun soll, noch erfahren!
>   (1074-76)

Rhymes gradually increase in the course of the play and are dominant in Act V when Maria receives absolution. Here we are clearly invited to correlate the stylistic containment of the rhyme with the spiritual composure of Maria — the text suggests that formal dignity underwrites Maria's moral regeneration:

> Es war der schwerste Kampf, den ich bestand,
> Zerrissen ist das letzte irdsche Band. (3690f.)

Or:

> So schenke mir die ewge Gnade Sieg
> Im letzten Kampf, als ich dir wissend nichts
>   [verschwieg. (3709f.)

It is noteworthy that Elisabeth is only granted one rhyming couplet. In her tortured and self-torturing monologue of IV,10 she defines the constrictions that determine her life, the imperatives of having to please the people; and these constraints are poignantly captured in the rhyme which combines the two poles of her life:

> ...einem Pöbel muß ichs
> Recht machen, dem der Gaukler nur gefällt.
> O *der* ist noch nicht König, der der Welt
> Gefallen muß!... (3195-98)

On one level then rhyme is the formal expression of a substantive centre, however bitterly negative it may be in the case of Elisabeth. However, on another level, it is also, in equal measure, to be found at prominent points of disorientation. One may of course argue in terms of traditional aesthetics that these cases perfectly illustrate the artistic achievement whereby shaping powers interlock with, yet contain a chaotic world. But the philosophical problem remains: if the formal dignity of the rhyme can be used to express loss of dignity, delusion, then we face those ambiguous values of form which Wilkinson perceives in Schiller when she speaks of 'a deep-seated ambivalence about the status of art and its relation to morality and philosophy' (*21*, p.223).[15] Rhyme is to be found in Mortimer's monologue of II,6 where we glimpse the first traces of his confusion, heightening the earthly Maria into a divinity:

Um sie, in ewgem Freudenchore, schweben
Der Anmut Götter und der Jugendlust,
Das Glück der Himmel ist an ihrer Brust,
Du hast nur tote Güter zu vergeben! (1648-51)

In III,6, as Mortimer's moral disorientation reaches frightening proportions, rhymes dominate:

Nichts blieb dir als die rührende Gestalt,
Der hohen Schönheit göttliche Gewalt,
Die läßt mich alles wagen und vermögen,
Die treibt dem Beil des Henkers mich entgegen —
(2571-74)

As we have seen in an earlier section, the motif of delusion is sounded at the start of III,1 where Maria expressly refuses to perceive, to acknowledge reality. Again, rhyme as an element of stylistic orientation is in the service of — overtly willed — disorientation, of 'süßen Wahn', which, tellingly enough, is interrupted by Kennedy's unrhymed discourse of reality. Maria rejoices:

---

[15] See also *20*, p.xli: 'For it was his fate, and his achievement, to illuminate out of the urgency of a felt conflict tensions which do in fact exist between beauty and virtue, grace and merit, the aesthetic and the moral.'

O Dank, Dank diesen freundlich grünen Bäumen,
Die meines Kerkers Mauern mir verstecken!
Ich will mich frei und glücklich träumen,
Warum aus meinem süßen Wahn mich wecken?

(2087-90)

And Kennedy warns:

Ach, teure Lady! Ihr seid außer Euch,
Die langentbehrte Freiheit macht Euch schwärmen.

(2105f.)

Perhaps the most disturbing case of rhyme is to be found in
V,10. Here, Leicester, in the 'Verzweiflung der Verdammten'
(3846), drives himself into the rhymed rhetoric of resolution:

Willst du den Preis der Schandtat nicht verlieren,
Dreist mußt du sie behaupten und vollführen!
Verstumme, Mitleid! Augen, werdet Stein!
Ich seh sie fallen, ich will Zeuge sein. (3857-60)

This language, in its discrepancy between forceful expression
and appalling lack of moral centre, is almost unbearable, and it
comes as a relief when the rhetorical stand finally collapses into
fragmentation and we are granted a moment, however fleeting,
of authenticity as we see Leicester 'plötzlich mit einer zuckenden
Bewegung zusammenfahren und ohnmächtig niedersinken'.
    As these examples illustrate, *Maria Stuart* is shot through with
caveats as regards the rhetoric which the characters and the play
itself employ. The built-in motifs of the spectacle and 'Suada',
the questionable dignity of expression, challenge us to bear in
mind that polished form *may* be transparent upon man's
potential to conquer primitivity — 'Herrschaft des Geistes über
seine Empfindungen' — but that fundamentally it is no
guarantee: 'Die Würde bezieht sich auf die Form und nicht auf
den Inhalt des Affekts' (*Ueber Anmuth und Würde*, NA XX,
pp.296-97).
    Once again it is worth noting that Schiller's aesthetic

deliberations tally closely with the historical context of *Maria Stuart*, that phase in European history when not open warfare, but the manipulation of the word was so decisive — that 'mass of negotiations and agreements made and broken' of which Elton speaks (*24*, p.295). More specifically, the Tudor Age, which created the supremacy of parliamentary statute, cannot yield that absolute certainty which the play's formal clarity seems to imply. Thus, the lexical and conceptual axis of 'richten', 'Recht', 'Gerechtigkeit' may be most prominent, but the imperative inherent in this central pattern cannot be fulfilled, given the fundamental uncertainties inherent in the Tudor Revolution. If, as Elton reminds us, 'in law and on earth there is nothing that an act of parliament cannot do' (*24*, p.168), then the order of norms and values can be but a relative one. Thus, for the historian Elizabeth's claim to the throne is no more than 'not a bad one, resting as it did on an act of parliament (1543) and Henry VIII's will' (*24*, p.269). In III,4 Maria devastatingly rounds on Elisabeth:

> — Regierte Recht, so läget *Ihr* vor mir
> Im Staube jetzt, denn *ich* bin Euer König. (2450f.)

but Maria's point is anachronistic — she invokes a traditional order which has long since been overtaken.

The text invites us to 'richten', and indeed we can judge, yet only on procedural grounds: the means by which Maria has been tried and convicted are indubitably corrupt. But we cannot judge substantively, neither as regards the conflicting claims to the throne nor in respect of the moral issue. Beneath the firm textual surface, Schiller's play anticipates in no small measure the perspectivism of a modern drama and the principle of relativity which historiography must adopt. Thus Bindoff writes of the moral dilemma in which Elizabeth found herself: 'Justice had long demanded that Mary should die, but it was expediency, not justice, that sent her to her death in 1587' (*23*, p.246). The characters, and indeed the play itself, may desperately invoke a stable system, but the norms and values at stake can be no more than relative.

Relativity and perspectivism can be seen at work even in linguistic details, in the use of such normative epithets as 'heilig'. Examination shows that the term, so frequently invoked, lacks a stable substantive centre: it is merely a functional extension of the characters' varying points of views. The 'heilig Recht' (1288) of Elisabeth's rule is not acknowledged by the Catholic viewpoint; Maria argues that her imprisonment transgresses against 'das heilge Gastrecht' (940) and that it is therefore her 'heilig Zwangsrecht' (946) to fight back. In III,4 Elisabeth refutes Maria's charge of having offended against 'des Gastrechts heilige Gesetze,/Der Völker heilig Recht' (2299f.) by countering that the Catholic church, which 'den Treubruch heiligt' (2355), absolves her of any such obligations. This totally secularized 'heilig' is seen at its nadir when, after the attempt on Elisabeth's life, Burleigh yet acknowledges Aubespine's diplomatic immunity, bowing to its 'heilige Charakter' (2668). As these examples illustrate, within the political sphere, the word is potentially or *de facto* devoid of meaning: in a world where each agent 'mit Verträgen spielt' (2694), the contract between word and substance is highly volatile.

The inherent devaluation of language is also, and most disturbingly, to be observed on the spiritual level. Take the terms 'Himmel' and 'himmlisch'. Maria greets any prospect of rescue as a heavenly sign. The parallel with Mortimer is overt: he perceives his mission as divinely ordained — 'Hört an, wie Euch der Himmel Rettung schickt' (406) — he sees himself as the instrument of 'Des Himmels wundervolle Rettungshand' (539). Similarly, Maria invokes God, the 'Wunder seiner Allmacht' (407), and encourages Mortimer, fully convinced that he has been sent by her 'guter Engel' (678). In III,1 Maria rejoices in the promise of freedom, hails the 'himmlische Luft', deeming herself to be divinely protected: 'Umfängt mich nicht der weite Himmelsschoß?' (2082, 2091). And when she panics at the news that she is to meet Elisabeth, she typically turns to Talbot for help: 'Vom Himmel mir ein Engel zugesendet!' (2172). Yet, all such instances are mere delusions. The phrases ring with bitter irony and their ramifications for Act V are profound: for here, on the most common reading, we find, as it were, the genuine article: Maria's ascent from the confusion of the phenomenal world into the purity of the transcendent realm. Schiller shapes the antithetical correspondences most carefully: Maria, who grasped the rescuing hands of Mortimer and Leicester, the illusory promise of 'des Himmels wundervolle Rettungshand' and 'Der Liebe tätge Hand' (2123), has now, according to Kennedy, been granted by God the strength 'glaubenvoll den Himmel zu ergreifen' (3408). And the figures of Mortimer and Leicester, the questionable saviours within Maria's physical prison, now yield to the figure of Melvil, the priest, who will, through the absolution and communion, liberate her from spiritual imprisonment. Maria greets him as the true 'Himmelsbote,/Da jeder irdsche Retter mich getäuscht!' (3663f.), he embodies 'ein himmlisch Glück' (3656).

The term 'Himmel' then covers a wide spectrum of meaning, extending from total delusion on the one hand to genuine revelation on the other. Faced with this problematical lexical constellation, the critic has a number of choices. At one extreme, one could hold that the negative reverberations undermine the positive value now ascribed to the term of 'Himmel'. On such a reading, the text even in this one specific respect enacts the impossibility of representing 'das Uebersinnliche', revealing itself as no more than 'süße Wahn'. At the other extreme, one may argue that even on a strictly lexical level Act V triumphs in Hegelian terms as an 'Aufhebung': that within the context of Maria's moral regeneration and the ritual of the sacrament the formerly problematic term 'Himmel' is annulled and yet preserved in the now higher state, that the tainted word itself is redeemed. But equally, we may take up that middle position which is so characteristic of Schiller's theoretical deliberations with all their built-in qualifications. On such a reading, the echoes of Maria's earlier delusion still reverberate, but they function as an illuminating, not destructive, relativizing force, alerting us once again to the sheer risks which the journey of both text and heroine entails. Sensuousness and its language, in the very act of yielding up to the metaphysical realm, may yet be entrapped in this world.

In my view, the strength of *Maria Stuart* rests precisely on the fact that within the brilliant clarity of its design we encounter the most tantalizing complexities. In acting out the problematic relationship between form and substance, the play captures the very centre of politics — in particular the mood and mode dominating that specific phase in the Elizabethan Age — and at the same time it yields a supremely fine critique of the status of art.

Conclusion

In the foregoing I have tried to suggest a range of thematic concerns — political, psychological, philosophical — which inform *Maria Stuart*. Above all I have sought to emphasize their complex interplay whereby we are constantly reminded of the overlap which obtains between the various spheres of human feeling, thinking and doing. It is one of the supreme achievements of this play that it compresses such density of argument into the brief compass of a tightly controlled artistic statement.

Yet I am aware that my analysis has ultimately uncovered levels of possible interpretations rather than a stability of meaning, that it has highlighted complexity rather than interpretative certainty. The upshot of my argument is not, however, that the play is devoid of meaning: *Maria Stuart* is clearly not some glittering conundrum. Nor would I take the line of Janz who perceives in *Die Braut von Messina* a discontinuity between Schillers's intention and the actual import of the text and argues that the play enacts the 'Demontage tragischer Größe', that 'mit der Erhabenheit des Helden entfaltet das Drama selbst auch deren massive Destruktion'.[16] But I do believe that the interpretative issues which *Maria Stuart* raises are symptomatic of Schiller's intellectual honesty which scrupulously traces those interconnections between the dictates of practical reality and the transcendent energies in man, be they moral or aesthetic. If none of these issues receives an unambiguous answer, this has to do with Schiller's refusal to cut corners, to take a short cut to certainty. And we owe it to an intelligence of this order that we too as interpreters abstain from short cuts. If I have been sceptical about Maria's transfiguration in Act V, this is not

---

[16] Janz, op. cit., pp.345-49.

because I wish to argue that her closing words are merely a further exercise in self-stylization. My argument is concerned to keep the short cuts of both the psychologically reductive and the metaphysical reading at arm's length. The totality of the play's meaning is not 'merely' one thing. Rather, the text alerts us to a number of possible interpretations as regards the images of human endeavour which it puts before us. It invites us to entertain those possibilities — but to entertain them knowingly, in full awareness of other, competing inerpretations. Schiller knew, perhaps better than anybody else, how aesthetic experience engages us not only sensuously and emotionally, but also reflectively. That reflectivity may sometimes allow us less certainty than we would ideally like, but it is this unceasing traffic of inquiry which is at the very centre of Schiller's *œuvre*.

Select Bibliography

CRITICAL WORKS ON SCHILLER

1. Ayrault, R., 'La figure de Mortimer dans *Maria Stuart* et la conception du drame historique chez Schiller', *Etudes Germaniques*, 13/14 (1958), pp.313-24.

2. Beck, A., 'Schillers *Maria Stuart*', in A. Beck: *Forschung und Deutung. Ausgewählte Aufsätze zur Literatur*, ed. U. Fülleborn (Frankfurt a.m., Athenäum, 1966).

3. Berman, J., 'Schiller's Mortimer and the Gods of Italy', *Oxford German Studies*, 8 (1973/74), pp.47-59.

4. Borchmeyer, D., *Tragödie und Öffentlichkeit. Schillers Dramaturgie im Zusammenhang seiner ästhetisch-politischen Theorie und die rhetorische Tradition* (Munich, Fink, 1973).

5. Graham, I., *Friedrich Schiller's Drama: Talent and Integrity* (London, Methuen, 1974).

6. Grawe, Ch., *Friedrich Schiller, Maria Stuart, Erläuterungen und Dokumente* (Stuttgart, Reclam, 1978).

7. Koopmann, H., *Friedrich Schiller*, 2 vols, Sammlung Metzler (Stuttgart, Metzler, 1966).

8. Kraft, H., *Um Schiller betrogen* (Pfullingen, Neske, 1978).

9. Mainland, W.F., *Schiller and the Changing Past* (London, Heinemann, 1957).

10. Sammons, J.L., 'Mortimer's conversion and Schiller's allegiances', *Journal of English and Germanic Philology*, 72 (1973), pp.155-66.

11. Sautermeister, G., 'Maria Stuart', in Hinderer, W. (ed.), *Schillers Dramen. Neue Interpretationen* (Stuttgart, Reclam, 1979).

12. ——, *Idyllik und Dramatik im Werk Friedrich Schillers. Zum geschicht-lichen Ort seiner klassischen Dramen* (Stuttgart, Kohlhammer, 1971).

13. Schlaffer, H., *Widerstände gegen Klassikerlektüre. Ein Unterrichts-modell zu Schillers Maria Stuart*, Projekt Deutschunterricht, 7 (Stuttgart, Bremer Kollektiv, 1977).

14. Seidlin, O., 'Schiller: Poet of Politics', in Willson, L. (ed.), *A Schiller Symposium* (Austin, University of Texas Press, 1960).

15. Sharpe, L., *Schiller and the Historical Character* (Oxford, University Press, 1982).

16. Stahl, E.L., *Friedrich Schiller's Drama: Theory and Practice* (Oxford, Clarendon, 1954).

17. Staiger, E., *Schiller* (Zurich, Atlantis, 1967).
18. Storz, G., *Der Dichter Friedrich Schiller* (Stuttgart, Klett, 1959).
19. Wiese, Benno von, *Die deutsche Tragödie von Lessing bis Hebbel (Hamburg, Hoffmann und Campe, 1961)*.
20. Wilkinson, E.M., and L.A. Willoughby, *Friedrich Schiller,* 'On the Aesthetic Education of Man in a Series of Letters' (Oxford, Clarendon, 1967).
21. Wilkinson, E.M., 'Schiller's concept of *Schein* in the light of recent aesthetics', *German Quarterly*, 28 (1955), pp.219-27.
22. Wilkinson, E.M., and L.A. Willoughby (eds), *Friedrich Schiller,* 'Kabale und Liebe' (Oxford, Blackwell, 1962).

HISTORICAL STUDIES

23. Bindoff, S.T., *Tudor England* (Harmondsworth, Penguin, 1985).
24. Elton, G.R., *England under the Tudors* (London, Methuen, 1967).
25. Neale, J.E., *Queen Elizabeth* (Harmondsworth, Penguin, 1971).
26. Pollard, A.F., *The History of England* (London, Williams and Norgate, 1910).